Glenn Exum

*To my Pal
"Cactus" Sherman
Gray.
With love
Glenn*

GLENN EXUM

Glenn Exum

"Never a Bad Word or a Twisted Rope"

A Collection of Climbing Stories by Glenn Exum
Compiled and edited by Charlie Craighead

Published by Grand Teton Natural History Association
Moose, Wyoming

ISBN 0-931895-52-9

Project compiled, edited, and coordinated by Charlie
Craighead.
Design by Carole Thickstun
Reviewed by Al Read, Sharlene Milligan and Bill Swift
Scanning by Pioneer of Jackson Hole
Printing by Precision Litho

*Anybody that had the good fortune to know
Glenn came away a better person.*

-Bill Briggs

Table of Contents

GLENN, BETH AND ED EXUM

Introduction

ONE SUMMER DAY IN 1931 a young college student stood poised on some precarious footholds high up on the Grand Teton in Wyoming. Ahead lay a gap in the ramp he had climbed up. On the other side of the two-thousand-foot abyss ran a wall of virgin rock that could prove to be too difficult for a first-year aspiring mountain guide. He pondered the consequences of a fall, wondered whether his football cleats would hold on the slick orange granite, and then he jumped.

The young music student, Glenn Exum, continued on that day to make the first ascent of the "Exum Route" and meet up with his mentor, Paul Petzoldt, on the summit. Over the next thirty years he safely led hundreds of clients to the summit of the Grand in the course of his more than 300 successful ascents. He failed to summit only once. In his modest style, Glenn claims his success came from being able to read the clouds and predict the weather. There had to be more to it than that.

The old-school Matterhorn guide would cajole and tug and swear until the client became more afraid of the guide than of the mountain. Glenn would also be firm, but his genius lay in taking the time and effort to allow the client to build confidence in his or her own abilities. What client would not trust a guide who was supremely confident himself—and was a dead ringer for Errol Flynn?

After he took over the Petzoldt-Exum School of American Mountaineering from Paul in 1956, he formed it into one of the most respected companies of guides in the world, now employing over fifty guides in a summer. It was Glenn Exum, more than anyone in America, who transformed mountain guiding from a summer job for itinerant climbers and college students into a genuine and respected profession. Some of his guides were veterans of Denali and Mount Everest, or El Capitan in Yosemite. Others had less impressive credentials. However, when Glenn stood outside the "guide shack" to introduce a group of clients to their guide, it was very clear that they were to be guided by one of the best climbers in the world.

I spent many summers climbing in the Tetons, from 1956 to the present. I never worked for Glenn though, Lord knows, many times I could have used the money. The "dirt bag" climber's life existed on the fringes of society — climbing hard and sleeping in an old CCC camp incinerator. A mainly oatmeal diet was supplemented with the occasional poached (not a cooking term) "fool's hen," marmot, or porcupine. On special days there was spaghetti with a can of cat tuna from the dented can store in San Francisco. My lifestyle and demeanor were less professional than that required by Exum Guide Service. In fact, I was on the outs with the Exums because of a little unauthorized guiding of Jackson Lake Lodge employees.

One day Glenn announced to his guides that perhaps I wasn't such a bad sort. He had seen me out in Lupine Meadows that morning enjoying the

GLENN EXUM   YVON CHOUINARD

beautiful sunrise. The truth was I had been staggering about barefoot, as usual, after an all-night Vulgarian rave at the climber's camp near "Guide's Hill."

Not long after that I was walking by the guides' shack when I saw Glenn teaching his son, Eddie, to fly cast. He invited me to join in and from that summer on I never went back to my spinning rod. Glenn was a beautiful fly caster and a dry fly fisherman. His favorite flies were the delicate light and dark cahills and the more gaudy Bob Carmichael's Mormon Girl. These would cover most of the limited hatches on the freestone Snake River. Eddie Exum became one of the best fly fishermen I've ever fished with. One of his notable accomplishments is a thirty-three pound steelhead taken on a dry fly.

Glenn sold the guide service to his four chief guides in 1982. It was after this date that I finally did get to work for the Exum Guide Service. I taught some special snow and ice courses and did some "overflow" guiding for a few years. That experience helped me to appreciate the skill and commitment it takes before one should accept the responsibility of putting people's lives into your own hands. I felt nothing but pride to be part of the profession and company of guides.

There was hardly a prouder time in my life than when I was honored to be asked to share a rope with Glenn on his last ascent of the Grand at age 71. Even then he climbed as elegantly as he fly fished — graceful, effortless, never breathing hard or clutching around. He was always under control.

The idea for this book came from Glenn. He has always been the storyteller. He has always been most alive and happy when story telling. Relating tales of his early Jackson Hole days to rapt young guides is his best relief from the constant pain of a debilitating illness.

At his home in Moose several years ago I read a few chapters he had written and I encouraged him to keep writing. I taped him for hours as he recounted, with amazing accuracy, the stories of his music and climbing careers.

Glenn's life is the story of a man who exemplifies Saint-Exupery's "Freedom is acceptance of responsibility." Glenn has always known that his role in life is to lead men.

—Yvon Chouinard

The only manly thing I could do was grab him by the left shoulder, turn him toward me and hit him as hard as I could on the jaw.

-XM

EXUM COLLECTION

GLENN EXUM IN 1929, AGE 18

PAUL PETZOLDT   GLENN EXUM

■ *In those days equipment was very sparse. We didn't have anything. Each of us had an old army blanket which we rolled up and then put around our shoulder and then tied it at the bottom, you know. Then we went up and stayed at the Petzoldt Caves at timberline, and Paul took me up the Grand, up the Owen Route. I was really impressed with his knowing the mountain.*   *-XM*

The Exum Ridge

PAUL HAD TAKEN ME UP THE **G**RAND **T**ETON the summer of 1930. I had finished high school and was going to Moscow to the University. Paul was going there too, so we continued our friendship in the winter. The next summer, in '31, we came out and I was playing in the band at Jenny Lake and working on the trail. One day Paul said, "Ex, I'm going to make a guide out of you."

I said, "This is rather sudden. I've never climbed except last summer with you, and I don't know anything about it."

He said, "That's all right. You have the aptitude."

"Why," I said, "I don't have any shoes."

Paul used to play center on the University of Idaho's football team, and when he invited me to go on this climb he said, "I have a pair of football cleats you can use."

The shoes were about two sizes too big, so I put on some extra socks. I didn't know any better at that time because I was young and quite agile. They were kinda like a pair of roller skates, but they must have gripped something.

Anyway, as we were going up the couloir on the way to the Upper Saddle, Paul said, "Ex, why don't you go over there, take a look at that ledge, and if you think it'll go, why go, and we'll meet you on top. If you don't think it will go, call me and we'll wait for you." Paul had seen the ledge from the top of the South Teton back in 1924, and once in a while from up there in the couloir.

That day the wind was blowing from the southwest and I got up there to the end of that ledge and it scared me, but when I called out to Paul, he couldn't hear me and didn't answer. I walked away from the ledge seven times, until I finally got up there and saw those little handholds and the boulder on the ridge. When you get to the eastern extremity of Wall Street, why, there isn't any place to jump from. So I climbed as high as I could until I was sorta secure, and I jumped from a standing start.

Once I got across there, I was mortified. Almost paralyzed. But I just decided that from then on I was going to change my whole attitude about it, because there was only one way to go, and that was up.

And you know, the other party was over on the ridge next to us, the Underhill Ridge, on that same day. And I

It wasn't planned that we went to Jackson Hole to climb a mountain. We were going there because we'd heard about outlaws and big trout, all the moose and elk and bandits and all of that. But when we saw those mountains, we didn't talk about it or anything, we were just going to climb them, that's it.

—Paul Petzoldt

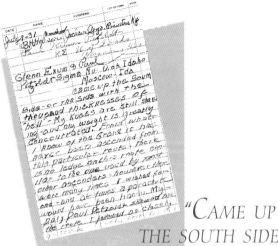

"Came up the south side—
or the side with the thousand
thicknesses of "hell" —My knees are
still shaking and my weight is greatly
concentrated. From what I know of the
Grand it has never been ascended from
this particular route—there is no ledge
on the route similar to the one used by
most other ascenders—however there
were many times I wished for one—
and at times a parachute would have
been handy. My pal, Paul Petzoldt
showed me the route.
I followed as closely as possible.
Lovely trip and here's hoping that
Fryxell, Underwood, Smith and the
other gent from Harvard come up her
mighty heights O.K. I could see them
working below and southeast—their
route is possibly more difficult than
mine—but I am hoping not for I can't
imagine much worse. I haven't my
watch but think it is 2 or 3 o'clock."*

–GLENN EXUM & PAUL PETZOLDT,
SIGMA NU U. OF IDAHO,
MOSCOW, IDAHO

Glenn's entry in Grand Teton Summit Register

■ *Paul Petzoldt and Glenn Exum with Mr. and Mrs. Fred
Wittenberger of Ohio and Austria, on July 14, 1931, the
day before they all climbed the Grand Teton and Glenn
ascended the Exum Ridge. It was Glenn's first guiding trip.*

was screaming at them just to get their attention, and they
never did yell back at me. Phil Smith, he said later, "I
thought you were over there just watching us."

And I said, "Hell no, I was over there trying to climb
the mountain, and I just wanted to talk to somebody but
you never answered." I think I was probably yelling
because I wanted to communicate with somebody. I was
really alone, but I thought if I could at least get in a word
with them, it might be some comfort, you know. It was
kinda crazy and I didn't know anything. My equipment
wasn't very good. I was wearing that pair of football shoes.
Finally I said to myself, "Well, I'm just going to climb and
quit talking." The fear left me and I just started floating
along. Just going.

I never saw Paul and the Austrians until he got clear to
the top. I had been sitting up at the top of the mountain
there about an hour and a half. I was looking off to the
south and Paul, he comes up from the west, and the first
thing I saw of him were those bushy eyebrows, you know,

and he saw me and he couldn't believe it. He said, "My God, Ex," and started to run, and he forgot the Austrians were attached to him. They were just little guys, hitting the rocks. And he came over there and gave me a big bear hug and said, "This is somethin' else. Do you know what you've done?" I had no idea about the significance of my climb at all. I didn't really know the history of the mountain. Nor did I have any idea that I was doing what I did. It was not mapped out, it was just something that happened, you know. I just happened to do it.

We all made it down to the Lower Saddle and I took off because I had to play in the band that night. Paul had gone to take a look at the route. I thought when he got out to the end of Wall Street I heard him holler down, "Any old lady could do this," you know, and that kinda made me mad, so I ran all the way down to Jenny Lake. Later I found out that he said, "Exum, you're crazy to do this."

GLENN EXUM   PAUL PETZOLDT, 1990

■ *Well, I think my friendship with Paul has been a very deep, sincere relationship. And it seems like when either of us sort of gets out of sync, why the other's always there to try to get us back in.*

—XM

5

"**NOWHERE IN THE HISTORY OF MOUNTAINEERING** has anyone received as much acclaim and notoriety for 20 feet of climbing as Glenn did. He faced a few feet of climbing that he wasn't entirely equipped for, nor had the training to do it. And he did it successfully. It was a fatal fall awaiting him if he didn't make it. The rest of the ridge that he climbed was very simple, and not anywhere close to the difficulties of going around the corner from Wall Street to the Ridge. Everyone thought he did a nice job and they really did it up around that — the movies and the rest of it."

———Jack Durrance

JULY 6: Dr. Fred Ayres of Evanston, Illinois, Keith Anderson of Rexburg, Idaho, Floyd Wilson and Will Thompson of Jackson, Wyoming ascended the Grand Teton by way of the southwest ridge and returned to their timberline camp by the Owen route of 1898 thus opening the 1937 climbing season. To reach the southwest ridge first developed by Glenn Exum of Pocatello, Idaho, it is necessary to follow along the exposed ledge on the face of a 2,000 foot buttress, and then to cross an intervening gash in the mountain by throwing a rope over a projecting rock on the far side. After crossing safely, the climber works up the ridge and follows the steep, broken skyline to the summit. Ayres reports that the party encountered no exceptional difficulties on the trip, and the weather and seasonal conditions on the peak were found to be excellent.

———Nature Notes, GTNP,
Autumn 1937

1936: The southwest ridge of the Grand Teton, also known as Exum's Route, was initiated this season by Mr. Wayne Thompson, an A.M.C. member who probably holds the old age record for the Southwest Ridge climb, Ranger Naturalist Allan Cameron, Jack Durrance of the Dartmouth Outdoor Club who acted as guide for the remainder of the season, and the guide, Paul Petzoldt. One of the most publicized ascents of the season was the climb of this ridge by Miss Margaret Fulton Spencer and Glenn Exum.

———Nature Notes, GTNP,
1936

JIM OLSON

THE SOUTH FACE OF THE GRAND TETON SHOWING THE
EXUM RIDGE ROUTE, PIONEERED JULY 15, 1931 BY
GLENN EXUM. GLENN HAD NO ROPE AND WORE PAUL
PETZOLDT'S OVERSIZED, LEATHER-CLEATED FOOTBALL
SHOES. A CURIOUS PETZOLDT SOLOED THE ROUTE LATER
THAT DAY, USING HIS ROPE TO LASSO A BOULDER ACROSS
THE GAP THAT GLENN HAD LEAPED.

EXUM COLLECTION

*Years later, the Austrians, Mr. and
Mrs. Fred Wittenberger, visit Glenn at
his guide service office.*

EDDIE, AIDELLE AND GLENN (AGE 6)

ONE THING I LIKED ABOUT MY PARENTS...they always let me fly free... do anything I wanted. When I was about six years old I used to just take off...we made a living by cutting wild hay and there were four girls and two boys and it was pretty slim pickings sometimes. I would tromp the hay down in the wagon. I remember sometimes they'd let me go over by the river and I had a big cane pole and I'd sit there and fish until I heard the "ping-pong" which was a three car train that came up from Pocatello every day at noon, and that told me it was time to go home.

-XM

MY FATHER was born in a little place near Jackson, Mississippi and his heritage was Scottish. Oliver Kinchen Exum. OK Exum. My mother's maiden name was Tolman. I was born in Topaz, Idaho, on June 24th, 1911.

-XM

GLENN'S SISTER, GRACIE EXUM, VOTED THE MOST BEAUTIFUL GIRL IN HOLLYWOOD

◼ *Me on the left, with my arm around my best friend. His name was Elgin Wilmore but we called him Sam. His twin brother was Ellis. We used to live near the railroad tracks out across the swamp where we would raise wild hay. The amount of money we made depended on the weather and the rain. I loved to fish even then. I used to go over on the Portneuf River. We used to go up to a place called Crystal Spring and really get into 'em.*
— *XM*

WHEN I WAS A KID IN POCATELLO *I used to fight in the ring some, and they called me Kid Exum. My mother made me a pair of shorts that had G.E. on the left leg, and I used to get in there and fight the kids, and I usually won. But whatever money we got was thrown in the ring after we fought. They called it a curtain raiser...sometimes we would make as much as fifteen or twenty dollars... a fortune at the time.* — *XM*

A Song Away from Jackson

I BEGAN STUDYING MUSIC when I was a freshman at Franklin Junior High School. I took saxophone lessons from J.C. Gardner, who was a professor at Idaho Tech, which later became the southern branch of the University of Idaho and eventually Idaho State University.

I practiced diligently and in my junior year, which was at Pocatello Senior High School, I placed first in the alto saxophone division in a state-wide music contest held in Boise. That year I was playing in a Dixieland band. We did jobs in Blackfoot, Pocatello, and in some other southern Idaho towns.

Early that spring the Warner Stone Orchestra from Pennsylvania came to Pocatello on tour. They had lost their tenor saxophonist, I tried out, and got the job. In late May after the close of our school year, we left Pocatello and after many one-nighters along the way, ended up at Jantzen's Beach in Portland, Oregon for the summer.

The following fall I decided that I was too young to continue touring. Before I returned to Pocatello, the orchestra was invited to play a "Battle of Music" with the Vic Meyer's Band at the Trianon Dance Hall in Seattle. The two orchestras were placed at either end of the hall and alternated playing. Audience applause was the prize for this competition. It was a great experience and we did creditably, but I felt Vic had the best outfit: he was an innovative person and had some startling ideas.

Vic had never dealt in politics, but because of a bet and some needling from his bandsmen, he decided he would run for mayor of Seattle. He was kind of a crazy guy.

That was during the advent of Mahatma Gandhi. Vic hired a goat, dressed up in a sheet, was barefoot, and rented a two-hole privvy on wheels. He marched along with a Dixieland Combo in a political parade with a sign saying, "Vic Meyers and his Ghanda Sheethouse." The throngs of people were screaming with laughter and seemed to be saying to themselves, "No one is going to vote for this crazy dude, so I'm going to give him my vote."

Well, Vic won the election, became mayor of Seattle, and later ran for and won lieutenant governor for the state of Washington. He held this post for many years, and was acclaimed the best lieutenant governor the state had ever had.

■ *At the University of Idaho we played two nights a week and made $12 a week. We were getting by quite well on $50 a month. The tuition for a semester was $80 then. One time at the JY Ranch a dude came up to me with a ten dollar bill, and he said, "Could you sing this song for me?" and I said, "Sure, I'll sing it," but I didn't know the words so I made them up. He didn't know them either and he gave me the ten bucks, which was like a fortune at the time.*

—XM

I FOUND THAT BECAUSE the University of Idaho was a certified school, that I could count some of the applied music I'd taken there when I was in high school toward my degree. Then I had a frat brother whose father was chairman of the school board in Kellog, Idaho. We were doing an annual pepband show at the University and he came down to see it. I had a couple spots in it, playing the alto sax and clarinet. We did a number of Paul Whiteman arrangements and for a college level band it was really very good. I was also featured as a vocalist, and Dr. Lindsey later invited me up to Kellog.

■ *I used to sing a lot, singing in front of the band and playing.* Sweet Sue *and* Call me Darling...*all the old ones.*

—XM

11

THE BLUE BUCKET BAND
RAY KELLY, HARRY WALDEN, BILL HAWKINS, XM, SID WALDEN, DON WOLF

I WENT TO SAN FRANCISCO IN THE FALL OF 1930 with Uncle Clarence and his wife Jessie. I tried to get a job there, and it was in the depression and, boy, there were no jobs there. And finally by the grace of God I got a telegram from the band of the University of Idaho offering me a job playing at the Blue Bucket Inn. I went up at mid-term. I started at the University of Idaho in the spring of 1931. I had a double major, in music and dramatic art. I graduated in 1934, and was offered the job as music director in the mining town of Kellog. I was only about twenty-three then, and I stayed for 37 years.

GLENN EXUM, SECOND FROM RIGHT

A Future Career Clipped

AFTER TOURING THROUGHOUT THE NORTHWEST with the Warner Stone Orchestra, I returned to Pocatello and joined the Musician's Union. When the school year ended in the spring of '29, the secretary of our union received a call from Ray McNab, who had a dance band in Jackson and needed a saxophonist. They offered me the job and I decided to give it a try.

To get to Jackson, I took the train to Victor, Idaho, and the Clay Seaton Bus over the Teton Pass to Wilson. The "bus" was actually a three-seated black Chrysler that looked like a funeral hearse. At the time, the road over the pass was dirt with occasional strips of gravel. It was crooked and steep. Clay had to stop his bus a number of times and put water in the radiator to cool it down. I remember it was hissing and steaming.

We arrived in Jackson on schedule and Ray met me at the bus stop. He had arranged for a place for me to stay. That afternoon we had a practice and the following evening played at the Rainbow Hall, just north of the town square. We each made six dollars from that gig, and then jobbed around at the dude ranches. Things were really pretty skimpy and I decided I had better get a day job.

One day soon after I'd set my mind to moonlighting, I was walking up Broadway, the main street, and noted a sign on the window of the town's only barber shop. It read, "Barber Wanted." I had clipped a little hair around home, assisting my four sisters and brother Eddie when they were shaggy. I went in the shop and surveyed the situation.

The owner was working in the first chair. There were two additional chairs and a line of five fellows waiting to be served. I spoke to the barber and said, "Sir, I'm a barber and looking for work."

He said, "Son, take the third chair and the fellow on the end of the line."

I was mortified when I looked at my client. He had about two month's growth of beard and wanted a shave. I really had no idea what I should do. I had observed the barber as he cranked his customer into the horizontal position after he had tied the cape on him. I put the cape on my fellow backwards and cranked him into the horizontal position. I looked down at him and thought, "My God, what do I do now?"

I noted a shaving mug with the the brush in it and I put a straight edge in my hand. I decided to give the brush a couple swirls in the mug, which quickly made a lather. I should have taken the electric clippers and clipped the face before shaving my hairy customer. I noted the barber stropping his razor before using it. I decided to give the straight edge a couple of swipes, and in so doing cut the leather strop in two.

I had the lather foaming on my client's face. I grabbed the razor and held it much like an Englishman would hold a cup of tea, extending the little finger as I held it. I looked down at my customer and by this time his eyes were rolled back and he was in a state of shock. Just as I prepared to take the first swipe the barber walked over to me, took the razor out of my hand and said, "Son, you had better let me finish him."

Had he not come to my rescue it is likely that I would have "finished" the hairy one. I put my coat on and walked out of the shop.

After telling my wife, Beth, of this incident years later, she said, "If you had been successful that day you might still be standing behind that barber chair."

JACKSON, WYOMING, 1930

■ *My first trip through Yellowstone was very memorable. It was in 1927 and I was on my Harley Davidson motorcycle with Ellis Wilmore. He sat on a little seat behind me. We didn't even have a windshield on it.*

-XM

GLENN WORKING AT HINES-GILLETTE
MOTOR COMPANY FOR $1 A DAY

Bedlam at the Jenny Lake Dance Hall

In May of 1930, the year I graduated from Pocatello High School, I was playing in a Dixieland dance band and had saved a bit of money. With it, I bought two new suits, and after the last day of school I immediately departed for Jackson to play in the Cliff Ward Dance Band. Cliff was not a musician but managed the band and all our bookings.

Our steady job that summer was at the Jenny Lake Dance Hall, and it was an exciting one. The cowboys, natives, and dudes would all meet there to whoop it up. Most of them could do the Jackson Hole Stomp, and when they got in sync with the band the old hall would actually rock. During that summer I had become a pal of Paul Petzoldt's, the first mountain climbing guide in the Tetons. He, in fact, took me on my first climb up the Grand Teton on the Owen-Spalding route in August of that year. We used to do a lot of fishing together and Paul would often come to the Jenny Lake Dance Hall.

Earlier in the summer I had met a delightful young lady by the name of Dorothy Redmond. She was from a well-established family in the valley who had a beautiful home at the east extremity of Antelope Flats. I used to put her gas in her car when she'd go up to the service station in Jackson where I was working. One day I asked Dorothy if she would care to go to the dance the next Saturday night. She said she would love to but had a problem: she had a friend visiting her from the University of Southern California. I suggested that Paul might like to come along and escort Dorothy's friend. I checked with Paul, who said he would be happy to if I would loan him one of my new suits. "Well," I said, "Which one do you want?"

He said, "I'll take the tweed."

We picked the girls up the night of the dance and arrived at the hall about thirty minutes before the dance started. I was in a rather awkward position, for I had to play in the band, but I arranged with Cliff Ward to lay out a few times during the evening so I could dance with Dorothy.

Paul did a super job entertaining the ladies while I played in the band. The second chance I got to dance with Dorothy, we were suddenly interrupted by John Emery, a big, brawny cowboy who was working at the Bar BC Ranch. I didn't know it at the time, but he was insanely in love with Dorothy. He stepped between us and said, "Dorothy, I want a dance!"

She said, "John, I don't want to dance with you."

He shouted, "I'll take this one!" He grabbed her arm and started waltzing away. The only manly thing I could do was grab him by the left shoulder, turn him toward me and hit him as hard as I could on the jaw. At his point, there was complete chaos in the dance hall. About five fellows grabbed me and tried to hold me, and I made sure they did. Others tried to subdue Emery.

In the meantime, Dorothy broke loose and ran to the south end of the hall. John was as strong as a bull and freed himself and ran after her. Roan Horse Smith was in charge of the evening lunch counter, which was situated in the

DOROTHY REDMOND, 1925

direction that Dorothy had run. Ronie had a little counter that was on hinges, which allowed him to lift it up and get behind the counter. Dorothy slammed through the counter and sprinted toward Ronie screaming, "Ronie, save me! He's after me!"

Ronie reached under the counter, pulled out a .45 Colt automatic and pushed the barrel into Emery's ribs. He was about to pull the trigger when John brushed Ronie's arm aside and pursued Dorothy. He caught up with her in the kitchen and hit her right between the eyes with his fist. Then he turned and stomped out of the dance hall.

During this fiasco, Cliff Ward had come up to me and said, "Exum, you get back up there on the bandstand and start blowing your horn." This is exactly what I didn't want to do, but after all, that was my job. I started blowing, but my heart wasn't in it.

Paul and the rah rah girl from USC had been outside looking at the stars. When Paul heard the hubbub he came to the bandstand and said, "Ex, where's the guy that hit Dorothy?" Emery had come back to the porch in the front of the hall and was leaning against the doorstep. Paul said, "Hold my coat." Well, it was my coat so I held it. Paul was in great shape and a superb athlete. He raced across the dance hall, winding up as he went, and when he reached Emery he hit him on the chin and knocked him off the porch. Paul bounded after him. Emery got up. Paul knocked him down again. Emery got up three times and the third time Paul really pounded him to the ground. This time Emery lay for a moment, turned on his left side and pulled out a knife with a blade abut eight inches long. There was a full moon and the blade reflected like a spotlight as he got to his feet. Five cowhands from the Bar BC overpowered him, threw him in the back of a truck and took him away.

The next morning while Paul and I were eating our breakfast at his camp at Jenny Lake, he received word that Emery was down in Jackson looking for him. Paul finished eating and said, "Ex, let's go on down. I want him to be sure he finds me." We got in Paul's old green Ford touring car and drove to Jackson. We inquired as to where Emery might be and were told that he was shooting craps at the pool hall across from the Joe Ruby Saloon. We walked in and sure enough, Emery was at the table throwing the dice. Paul walked over to the table, shouldered Emery out of his place, grabbed the dice and said, "I want to play." And old Emery, he just backed off and left the pool hall. We didn't see him again. He seemed to disappear and was not heard of for several years.

During that time Dorothy had met a handsome young cattle rancher from Montana by the name of Fernie Hubbard. She and Fernie were married and returned to Jackson for a short visit, renting a tenthouse at the edge of town.

One day Dorothy went to run some errands and Fernie was alone at the tent house. No one knows how John Emery got back to Jackson, but there he was. He had heard about Dorothy and Fernie, and decided that if Dorothy wouldn't have him, she wasn't going to have anyone. Fernie had his shirt off and was shaving with his back to the door, using a straight-edge razor. Emery opened the door and shot Fernie in the back. By the grace of God, the wound was not fatal, and Fernie recovered, and he and Dorothy lived a long, happy life raising cattle in Montana.

The natives of Jackson just didn't know what happened to John Emery. He seems to have disappeared again as he had done so many years earlier. Legend says that he was killed in a brawl; others say he spent the rest of his life in the penitentiary. I just don't know. I do know that I shall never forget that moonlit night at the Jenny Lake Dance Hall, and Paul wearing one of my new suits.

■ *I didn't know what I was doing, if I'd known about John Emery, even with a little bit of Van Gogh's hooch that we drank out on the lawn, I wouldn't have, because everybody was afraid of him. The deputy sheriff was there, and other people were there, and nobody was saying a thing to John Emery.*

But after that night, Madden Gabby, who was a representative in the state legislature, he took me aside and said, You are either going to have to leave the country or you've got to have a showdown with John. He's saying all over the valley that he'll kill you on sight. And so you've got to have a showdown or out. And Glenn didn't know this, but Gabby went in his back room and got his six shooter and stuck it in my pocket. He said, You keep this on you all the time. He makes a move, you shoot him. 'Cause he's gonna get you.

So we went down to the pool tables, Glenn didn't know that I had this six-shooter in my pocket. That's why I was brave.

—PAUL PETZOLDT

Beer

MANY YEARS AGO, when Paul Petzoldt was a young guide, he used to carry a pack of beer to the summit of the Grand Teton. On warm days, after reaching the summit, he would sit on the highest point of the mountain, rub his hands and exclaim, "I would give ten bucks for a good cold can of beer."

Sure enough, on every occasion, some unsuspecting client would reply, "So would I." Old Petzoldt would smile and wink, then reach into his cache, produce the beer, and collect the ten.

■ *1929, that was the year the Grand Teton National Park was dedicated. I rode up one day and saw the mountains and was really inspired. I went to the dedication of the park. Sam Woodring was Superintendent.*

■ *In 1930 I decided I'd like to get a job in the park, so I went up there and got a job working on the trails, which started at Jenny Lake and went clear up into Garnet Canyon. That summer I met Paul Petzoldt. We were all sleeping on the floor of an old cabin that Hank Crandall had brought down from his homestead. There was Phil Smith and Archie Teater, the artist, and Paul Petzoldt and myself, all sleeping in that old place. I was working on the trail and Paul was doing a little guiding when he could get a client. Paul and I became friends and he invited me to go up the Grand Teton with him, and in August we climbed the Owen Route.* -XM

18

Beavertooth Neal of Elk, Wyoming

AFTER PLAYING AT THE RAINBOW HALL the summer before, in 1931, the band moved up to the Jenny Lake Dance Hall, which was just north of the Jenny Lake Store and cabins owned by J.D. Kimmel. We also jobbed around the valley, playing at dude ranches like the White Grass, the Bar BC, and the JY.

On several occasions we played at the Charlie Neal Dance Hall at Elk, a rural area east of Moran. Charlie was better know as Beavertooth by his many friends. He was given that moniker because he had an unusually large overbite and resembled a beaver. He was a humorous fellow. He was tall and gangling and there was always laughter about him.

Beavertooth loved to dance and his patrons would always stay to watch him dance the last dance of the evening, which he saved for his daughter. His friends would clear the floor and allow him and his daughter plenty of room to swoop and sway. The crowd would applaud and scream in delight and finally join the two as the band played its farewell song, "Home Sweet Home."

Beavertooth not only looked like a beaver, he loved to trap them. He did it to such an extent that he finally got in bad with the law, was arrested and summoned several times to a trial in Cheyenne. Legend has it that he would set his traps on the way to the trial and pick up the pelts on his way back home. During his absence, his wife would suddenly be called to visit her sick mother in St. Louis. When she went she would take her large trunk, which would be tightly packed with the pelts that Beavertooth had garnered on his way home from his latest trial.

I found Charlie Neal to be a fine man, and we in the band were always honored whenever asked to play at his dance hall in Elk, Wyoming.

CHARLIE "B" NEAL

Black David, My First Car

Sɪᴅ Wᴀʟᴅᴇɴ ᴀɴᴅ I ᴍᴀɴᴀɢᴇᴅ ᴛᴏ ꜱᴀᴠᴇ a few dollars and thought it would be fun to go to a car auction. There was an exciting auctioneer and a large crowd. In jest, Sid and I started bidding on cars, knowing that someone would always overbid us. Such was not the case.

The car that was on the block was an old Davis touring car with a Redseal Continental motor in it. The auction started at twenty; someone bid twenty-five; we bid thirty. Another bid thirty-five; we bid forty. The auctioneer screamed, "Do I hear forty-five?" No answer. He waited just a moment and shouted, "Going once, going twice, sold to the young gentlemen for forty dollars."

We emptied our pockets, paid for the car, received the bill of sale, and rode away in great hilarity. Sid was driving. We made a swing up to the campus and to our fraternity house, showing everyone our new prize. The old car proved to be a very good one and Sid and I had many fun times in it before the semester ended.

Both Sid and Harry graduated in early June. They lived in Bonner's Ferry, which is in the extreme northern part of the state, and I lived in Pocatello. "What should we do with the car?" I asked.

Sid said, "Let's match for it." We threw up two coins.

I countered, "I'll match you." I did, and the car was mine. We shook hands. Sid and Harry went north, I found a group of students who needed rides to southern Idaho, and we headed for our respective homes. The car, Black David, functioned very well. I spent a couple of days in Pocatello, then headed for Jackson where by that time I was working with Paul Petzoldt as a guide, as well as playing for dances at the old Jenny Lake Dance Hall on Saturday nights.

BLACK DAVID

A Pitch-Black Bushwhack

ONE SATURDAY AFTERNOON Jackson residents Phil and Dorothy Smith invited me to their cabin for dinner. They lived east of Jenny Lake about six miles at the old LePage place, down a steep dugway and not far from the Snake River. I arrived at the cabin in good style, and had an elegant dinner with them. It was getting late and I was due to play in the orchestra at the Jenny Lake Dance Hall at nine o'clock. Just as I started up the dugway the sky blackened, lightning flashed across the sky and thunder rolled. In a few moments it was pitch-black and I was winding my way across the sagebrush flat.

At that time the upper Bar BC was farming a large tract of land east of Timber Island and there were a number of irrigation ditches, some running across the road. In these places, the irrigators had placed plank bridges across the ditches. I was purring along and making very good time when all of a sudden the car stopped. I looked at the gas gauge and it registered empty. I had hit a protruding spike that extended through one of the planks as I crossed the bridge, and punched a hole in the gas tank.

There was absolutely no traffic on that road and I knew I was in trouble. The moment I turned off the lights it was as black as the inside of a cow. I couldn't see my hand in front of my face. It was so dark I had no idea in which direction I was walking. I thought I was walking due west, but wasn't sure.

I was stumbling through the darkness when I finally heard running water. It was so dark I couldn't see the stream. I had no idea how large it was, so I got down close to the water and tried to determine the width of the stream by the sound of its flow. I decided it wasn't too wide and I thought I could jump it. I went back about fifteen feet, ran as fast as I could, and jumped.

I was right, but misfortune grasped me, for I had jumped into a barbed wire fence. I was thrown back into the water. I got up, slithered around in the water, crawled out on the bank and through the fence and finally got to my feet. There was something warm running down my leg. By this time I was completely disoriented, with no idea in which direction I was headed. I turned around three times and started to walk.

EXUM COLLECTION

■ *Phil Smith was one of the temporary rangers when the park first opened. He was a really funny guy. He lived up at Moran a few winters, and he said it would get so cold there that he would get up and take all the carpets from the floor and put 'em on the bed, and the rugs and everything. He said you could throw a cat through the chinking of his cabin. He said he'd set the alarm for two-thirty in the morning and get up and get some rest, and then go back to bed.*

—XM

After several hours I saw some lights which were on the highway running north to Jenny Lake. The lights were moving so I knew it was a car. I upped my tempo and came out on the highway just south of Timber Island. Another car finally came along and took me to the dance hall.

I arrived just as the orchestra was playing the finale, "Home Sweet Home." Cliff Ward, the gentleman who ran the dance hall and for whom I was working, was really excited. He looked at me, surveyed my disheveled state and said, "I contacted Dr. Fryxell and the rangers and they were getting ready to send out a search party."

I looked down at myself, saw the blood and torn clothing, and believe me, thought it was good just to be back at the hall.

1932. GLENN EXUM, BARBARA GRAY (FIRST WOMAN TO CLIMB NEZ PERCE), AND PAUL PETZOLDT.

■ *I stayed on and worked with Paul 1932, '33, '34, '35, '36, '37, '38. Well, in 1935 I went to Europe. I climbed the Matterhorn in 1935. That fall I came back and Paul and I took Betsy Cowles up the East Ridge, which was the third time it had been climbed. In 1938 Paul went to K2 and I went back to England.*

-XM

Why the Englishman Did Not Climb the Mountain

EARLY IN THE 1930S, an Englishman came to our headquarters and made reservations to climb the Grand Teton with me. He was a Colonel in the Grenadier Guard and looked the part; he had the traditional sandy moustache and quick-moving toddle of the Englishman. The colonel seemed to be fit and enthusiastic, and was technically a good climber. He had spent several days in the valley and was well acclimatized.

The evening before we were scheduled to start our ascent, the Colonel came to me in a state of frustration. He talked a good deal faster and his voice seemed to portray that of a North Englander; there was a definite dominance of Cockney as he expounded, "My dear Exum. I'm so very sorry I can't make the climb with you. As you know, I 'ave my wife with me. I 'ave my cat and worst of all I 'ave my dog. At the moment, she is in peculiar circumstance. You know, just as sure as I try to climb that blasted mountain, some 'alf breed American dog will come along and take advantage of her." He did not go on the climb.

There have been volumes written on why men climb mountains, but I have always thought the Colonel's reason for not climbing was indeed unique.

GLENN CLEANING HIS HOBNAILS. AT A SHOE LAST IN THE CAMPGROUND, ALL THE CLIMBERS POUNDED IN THEIR OWN "HOBNAILS."

■ *The roads were all dirt then. I remember one time Petzoldt and I were going to town and we got behind a guy and he wouldn't let us go past him, and it was so dusty and everything, so finally old Paul he saw an opening and he got right up and crowded the guy right out into the sagebrush. And then we just kept on going.*

We had our tire tubes along, and if you had a flat, why you'd just take the tire off and patch it and put it back on. Fix it yourself. If you went very far, you always expected to have a couple flat tires, you know.

-XM

MIKE BREWER, GLENN EXUM AND DICK POWNALL

■ **PAUL HAD THE GUIDING CONCESSION** after the war. The climbing was pretty much closed during the war...I think Phil Smith may have taken some people. Paul was in the Army 10th Mountain Division. I went down to Spokane and took the exams and qualified, and was going in the 10th Mtn. Division also, but my kids and bands were entertaining those who had been drafted, and they told me to stay on there instead of going into the army. So I stayed on the home front, but I joined the Idaho National Guard. I never did go into the armed services. I wish I had.

I remember how livid Billy Owen used to get when he would quote Langford, "Exposure to the winds kept it free from snow and ice, and its bald, denuded head was worn smooth by the elemental warfare waged around it." I recall how Fryxell and Phil Smith used to calm him down and give him a drink of water at that point so he could continue his lecture on the 1898 ascent of the Grand Teton.

-XM

Owen was not a villain, but a lovable old gentleman whom many of us admired, in spite of eccentricities, and growing senility. I didn't agree with all that Owen said, but I did feel that he was thoroughly honest. To me a controversy was a thing to be avoided, but to Billy it was a challenge! I didn't like the way outsiders would draw him out into extreme statements that they later used against him. It just wasn't fair to treat the old man that way.

-Letter to Exum from Fryxell

24

ROBERT UNDERHILL, BILLY OWEN, FRITIOF FRYXELL, GLENN EXUM

■ **HANK CRANDALL,** who was the park photographer, and I got that group together. Hank took a picture and then I gave him my camera. At that time the picture represented every route that had been climbed on the Grand Teton. Dr. Underhill, on the left, was the first to do the East Ridge, in 1929, and then he and Fritiof Fryxell did the North Ridge just a few days after he did the Underhill Ridge, which was the same day I did the Exum Ridge. And Billy Owen did the Owen Route.   –XM

I've thought about it a lot and studied it, and I'm convinced that Billy Owen was the first to climb the Grand Teton.

GLENN, BILLY OWEN

—XM

EDDIE EXUM

■ *My brother Eddie was an All American basketball player, Montana champion horseshoe pitcher, a great fisherman and wonderful singer.*

-XM

BETH EXUM

■ *I used to play the guitar and my brother Ed would sing. Back in 1938, '39, this guy says, "You guys better go out to Hollywood." So he set up a date for us to be tested with the RKO studios in Hollywood. Beth didn't know anything about this. So she went down to Hollywood with me and we took these tests.*

And Beth said, "You can either have Hollywood or me."

I said, "I'll take you."

-XM

■ **I HAD THAT SAME OLD CHRYSLER WHEN ED AND I** drove to Hollywood, and the first time we went out into that Mojave Desert we thought that if we put the windshield down flat it would make it cooler, but it almost cooked us in that hot wind. Then I said, "Ed, we're on the Arizona border on our way to Hollywood, and I'll tell you what. I'll run you a foot race...a hundred yards." Well, I used to run like a deer and I really took off and I was a couple of yards ahead and then he got his second wind and came flying by me like I was standing still. And then to think he'd go down there and take the screen test, and later die of spinal meningitis. I pray for Eddie every night.

EDDIE EXUM

GLENN EXUM

EDDIE WAS IN A COMA, and I was there in the hospital room with my brother-in-law, who was a professor of theology at UCLA. I was sitting there holding Eddie's hand. He had been in the coma for a long time. And he suddenly opened his eyes and looked at me and he says, "How's your hair?"

And I said, "Eddie, my hair's just fine." When I was younger I used to have a lot of hair and I was losing it, you know, and that's why he asked me that.

And then he said, "You know, I was on a ship and there were a lot of gobs on that ship, and I asked the Lord if I could go back and see my brother Glenn, and he said, 'Okay Ed, you may go. You may stay as long as you wish.'"

And so he came back and I must have talked to him for thirty or forty minutes, and then he looked at me and squeezed my hand and died. There's no love like a brother's love.

Old Petzoldt and I would go fishin', 'course he never wore waders. He just went out. And old Paul, he didn't have a net, so he was using his hat for a fish net. He would just take his hat off and get the fish in the hat.

I started fishing in northern Idaho a long time ago. My brother was a great fisherman, and he used to fish with Bob Carmichael, the legendary fisherman in Jackson Hole. I had a chance to fish with them and learned a lot of things from them.

-XM

FISHING ON LEIDY LAKE WITH SHERMAN GRAY. *We caught 87 fish in one day and kept two. We built a raft of old mining ties and wire, then went on to Hidden Lake and I set up Sherman with the worst fishing gear -- an old cane pole and an ugly fly -- since he was a terrible fisherman and I didn't want to waste good gear on him. But on his first cast Sherman caught a 7 1/2 pound cutthroat. On the second cast he did the same. We wrapped them in leaves and ponchos and tied them on the saddles, then rode all the way back to Moose and Sherman's mother roasted them.*

-XM

■ **I'VE FISHED WITH GLENN A LOT.** In fact, when I was first out in the Tetons I used to fish but I'd go out with worms or with spinners...I didn't know much about fishing. I remember one day in front of Glenn's house in the guide shack, he taught me how to flycast right there, and that got me started in flyfishing. Glenn is a great fisherman. He's an absolute purist...a dry fly fisherman. He won't use anything but dry flies, won't use nymphs or streamers. He's a really nice caster, very elegant. He sorta fishes like he climbed...he was a very graceful climber, effortless; never, ever breathing hard or clutching around. He was always completely under control, and I think he fishes the same way. I think he likes the elegance of flyfishing.

—Yvon Chouinard

Too Far to the Mountain

In the late 1930s there were two young men working at the Upper Bar BC Ranch on the bench above the Snake River. They were employed to irrigate the alfalfa, and they had a lot of time to contemplate things. Each day they would gaze up at the Grand Teton, which loomed into the sky far above them.

One Sunday morning they went to the kitchen and asked the cook if she would make them a couple of sandwiches. "We're going to climb the Grand Teton today," they told her.

They drove their car over to Jenny Lake and parked in Lupine Meadows. They started up the game trails which led to timberline and appeared to lead to the summit of the Grand. At sundown they found themselves on the ridge above Amphitheater Lake and pushed on for the summit of the Grand. But of course they reached Disappointment Peak, and they were in complete awe as they viewed the deep chasm that stretched between them and the East Ridge of the Grand Teton. They decided to retreat to the ranch.

They reached Lupine Meadows just as the moon was coming up and arrived back at the Bar BC just before midnight. The following day they were back working in the fields. Their confidence was gone. Soon after lunch they came to the most easterly ditch, which was full of water. Before their humbling attempt on the Grand they would have leaped in and waded the ditch, but now they halted and pondered the potential depth of the water. Then one of them completely disrobed, stepped to the edge, and said, "I'm not taking any chances. I'm going to swim 'er."

■ *I used to go out there and get my chainsaw and cut firewood up, and the rangers didn't seem to mind. But that was before they got concerned about it. We used to have fires on Mt. Moran. We had a fireplace up there.*

-XM

When the morning light came onto the mountain I heard someone yell, "Achtung!" The portly German ahead of me ducked as a rock about the size of a watermelon fell off the ridge above us.

-XM

I took a Picture and It Changed my Life

DURING THE SUMMER OF 1934 I had the pleasure of meeting the Dean of Windsor, Sir Albert Baillie, Chaplain to the King of England. He was a guest at the Triangle D Ranch, a private ranch north of the present Teton Village, owned by Prentis and Laura Sherman Gray. Paul Petzoldt and I were friends of the Grays, and one day they invited me to come along with them as they showed the Dean our western town. Jackson was budding at that time. There were only six businesses, each wisely placed around the Town Square.

We visited all six and ended up at Bruce Porter's drug store, on the square's east side. He had a buckrail fence in front of his store with a stuffed bucking horse mounted on it. Bruce had a professional photographer there and for twenty-five cents would rig you in chaps, spurs, beaded gloves, and a big hat, place you on the bronco and take your picture. I was the first to have my picture taken and Dean Baillie was next. Dressed in full attire, he gamefully straddled the bronc. The pro took his picture and I, by the grace of God, took one, too, with my old Eastman camera which had the bellows on it that had to be pulled out before it would function.

It turned out that taking the picture was a great break for me. The pro's photo did not turn out. Later that summer, after I returned to Kellog, Idaho, where I was the supervisor of music in the public schools, I set up a dark room and developed the roll of pictures I had taken in Wyoming. By crux of good faith, the photo of the Dean was perfect. I enlarged it and mailed it to him with a letter. I wasn't sure he would remember me. Less than a week later I received an airmail letter from the Dean, in which he replied, "Yes, I do remember you very well. Why don't you come and spend some time with me at the Deanery at Windsor?"

I responded immediately and told him it would be impossible for me to come, for I was teaching school. His quick reply suggested I come after my school term ended. I did some checking into finances and travel arrangements, and wrote that I would come. Again he responded promptly, saying to let him know when he should meet me at the Waterloo Station in London.

■ **PAUL AND I**, one time, we were going over to Gibb Scott's place, he was living with Miss Hunt, you know, the countess, and we were in the kitchen and Paul said, "The kitchen stove's got up and walked outside." Well, what actually happened was Wilma the cook was leaning in front of the stove, and she was bigger than the stove, and when she walked outside...well, that's what happened. But anyway, we went down to Wilson as always on Saturday night. I wasn't playing that particular Saturday night. And I said, "I'm going to dance with Wilma." Paul said, "You're nuts, you wouldn't dance with her." She weighed 345 pounds. I said, "You watch me." So I got out there and by golly, she was just like a cork in the ocean, you know. So graceful. And we were stomping around there, doing the Jackson Hole Stomp. And pretty soon a line formed and nobody could get a dance with Wilma.

CLARENCE MOORE, GLENN EXUM, BARBARA GRAY, PAUL PETZOLDT, BOB'S GIRLFRIEND, BOB LOENSTEIN.

■ **IN THE EARLY 1930S** Bob's father was the richest man in the world. Glenn took Bob up the Owen Route, and in 1935 met him in London to watch his polo team play India.

CLARENCE MOORE AND BOB'S GIRLFRIEND. BOB BOUGHT THIS CAR FROM MOVIE STAR ANNA MAE WONG, AND DROVE IT TO THE TETONS.

■ *I taught him how to climb and guide, but Glenn was an asset to me, too. He was playing at orchestras and had better clothes than me. It was a good way for me to go to dances and meet girls. We were invited because we were two guys who were more acceptable than some of the local cowboys. I've always had a very strong emotional attachment for Glenn, and it might have been because we had similar backgrounds. I came here as a homeless kid. He was more of a brother to me than any of my brothers.*
　　　　　　　　　　　　　—Paul Petzoldt

33

A Road Trip in Genevieve

THE SUMMER I MET THE DEAN in Jackson, a young friend of his, Englishman Christopher Leigh Smith, sold me a beautiful Imperial 80 Chrysler Roadster. It was a stroke of luck for me; Smith and the Dean decided to fly rather than drive back to New York and asked me to buy the car for the inexpensive price of $350. I had saved a little money from guiding that summer, so paid cash for it. She was beautiful; I named her Genevieve.

The following spring after school closed I drove Genevieve to New York, where I planned to catch a ship to England. I drove through Montana and then into South Dakota. While crossing that state, cruising along at about sixty miles per hour, a prairie chicken flew into my car and lodged between the fender and the headlight. It was killed, but not badly crushed. I picked it up and thought what a shame it would be to throw it by the roadside.

In a field to the left of the highway was a fellow plowing. I walked up to him and spoke to him, but he could not understand English. He was an Italian. I tried to explain what had happened in sign language, but he could not comprehend the message. Finally, I handed him the chicken and walked to my car. Before I drove away, I looked back to the knoll where he was standing. He was silhouetted against the sky, his arm extended, staring at the chicken. I hope he took his prize home and shared it with his family.

Before I left Kellog, I had decided that I would stay at the best known hotels along the way, as long as I could afford to do it. In Chicago, I stayed at the Stevens Hotel. As I came out of that city along Michigan Avenue, driving at about fifty mph, a traffic officer whistled me down and said, "Bud, you had better speed it up or they'll run over you." I did, and they didn't.

In New York I stayed at the Waldorf Astoria. The room cost me eight dollars. My uncle Clarence Tolman, who was blessed with a beautiful tenor voice and a handsome visage, had worked his way from the hills of Idaho to Broadway. In New York he performed with the Schubert Show Company and once sang the lead in the opera Countess Maritza. My uncle had encouraged me to come out and see Manhattan some day. There I was and I decided to get my car out of the parking lot and drive down and see the lights of Broadway.

I put Genevieve's top down and flattened the windshield, which was designed to be lowered to a horizontal position. The bright lights, neon signs and all the sparkle enthralled me. It was a cloudless night, the moon was full and the stars spangled from the heavens. I was overcome by the beauty of it all.

Suddenly I heard the screeching of tires and a shrill whistle. In my departure from this planet I had run through a stop sign, and an opposing vehicle running at high speed had missed me by about one coat of paint. A police officer blew his whistle again, stomped up to me and shouted, "What's da matter wid ya bud? Are yah blind?!"

I said, "Officer, I'm very sorry."

He was livid, and screamed, "We've got a guy done here dat's gettin' ten tousand dollars a year fer guys like you dat's sorry!"

I replied, "Officer, I'm still sorry."

His face flushed and he screamed, "Bud, which part of da city are yah from, anyway?!"

Again I answered softly, "Officer, I am not from the city."

"Well, where da hell are yah from?"

My answer was firm, "Officer, I'm from Idaho."

He stomped to the back of Genevieve and gazed at my license plate, which had an Idaho potato on it. When he sauntered back he was a changed man. He put his arm around me and cooed, "Son, take it easy. Dey'll kill yah." Had my Idaho potato not shown so vividly I'm sure I would have been fined and thrown in the brig. Thank God for Idaho potatoes.

After my adventure in New York, I drove to Dennsville, New Jersey, and left Genevieve with my pal Gus Koven's mother, before setting sail for England.

GLENN EXUM BOUND FOR EUROPE ABOARD THE DEUTSCHLAND (TWIN SCREW MAIL STEAMER).

CAPT. HEINRICH DEPARTED FROM NY THURSDAY JUNE 6, 1935 TO HAMBURG VIA SOUTHAMPTON

The Dean of Windsor at Waterloo Station

I HAD BOOKED PASSAGE on the German shipping company Nordeutcher Lines, which sailed out of the New York City harbor. It took seven days to cross the Atlantic before we docked in South Hampton, England. From there I took a train to London, where the Dean met me at Waterloo Station.

When the Dean was in Wyoming, he'd dressed in civilian attire. Now he was clergically clad. He wore a broad black hat, a clergical collar, a black shirt and jacket, knicker length trousers, black shoes with silver buckles, and carried a cane. He was a big man, very handsome and, in spite of his years, carried himself in a stately manner. His chauffeur met us with the Dean's car. The Dean was such a gracious man, and of course everyone seemed to know him. He made me feel very comfortable. He also made me wonder if I was up to being his guest at the Deanery at Windsor Castle; I certainly am no Saint and thought as I looked at him, that I must be on my best behavior and never do anything that would cause him discomfort.

I had never been anything but a social drinker, but was wondering if even that was considered appropriate to the Dean. I felt more comfortable after he offered me several choices of alcoholic beverages for lunch. After our meal we drove through the gate in the stone wall encircling the castle. I wondered if it was really me in that incredible situation. The area radiated with a grandeur that any child would imagine a fairyland to be.

We approached a round tower and continued on to the Dean's home, which was adjacent to St. George's Chapel. We went to the main door of the Deanery and entered. The rooms were conveniently arranged; there was a spacious dining area, a parlor with a grand piano, a library with a fireplace mantle studded with cameos and statuettes, a fire in the hearth, and the Dean's special chair adjacent to it, where he sat, read, and contemplated.

I was assigned a room that Anne Boleyn had stayed in when she was just a girl. Her uncle, Canon Samson, later became the Dean of Windsor. He liked Anne and gave her a special room in the Deanery. She was in that room, sitting near the window, when Henry the Eighth first sighted her. He was walking through the cloister of St.

EXUM COLLECTION

DEAN OF WINDSOR

The Dean always used to take a slug of scotch right before going to bed. And I knew a lot of German folksongs, so it got to be our custom that he'd take his scotch and we would skip up the stairs of Windsor Castle to our bedrooms, singing German folksongs.

—XM

George's Chapel and there she was. He fell in love with her, married her, but later had her beheaded at London Tower.

Hector Bolitho, a young man from Auckland, New Zealand, was also staying at the Deanery. The Dean introduced him to me one day and said, "He came to spend a weekend with me and stayed for five and a half years."

Hector was a writer whose books include The Romance of Windsor Castle, a number of novels and a biography of Edward the Eighth, who in 1938 abdicated at St. George's Chapel. Hector, who had almost finished his biography, changed the last chapter, published it and became wealthy. He later wrote the biography of George the Sixth, who was the Duke of York during Edward's reign. Hector was a scholar of English history and had funny stories to tell, including one about the young Prince of Wales, Edward the VIII.

When the young boy was learning the history of the Tudor Kings, his instructor told him for the first time about the number of wives King Henry the Eighth had. It is said that just as the awful truth was revealed to the prince, the Queen appeared at the door. The young prince whispered to his tutor, "Don't tell Mother about Henry the Eighth. She would be shocked."

At Windsor I read copiously and hiked the King's Garden, the Great Park and the Long Walk that extended far beyond the castle walls. I would go to the grounds of Eaton College just below the castle and watch the young students play cricket. On Sunday afternoons, I went to the area in front of the east apartment where the royalty stayed when they came down from Buckingham Palace. There would be simultaneous band concerts and the Queen would often come to the balcony and extend her hand to the people who stood enjoying the music.

Occasionally I would go to the King's private golf course. The Dean arranged for me to have a key that unlocked the wrought iron gate. There was always a full uniformed grenadier guard, Bear Shako and all, standing in a cupola. I would wink at him but there was no response. He would stand there at attention, rifle over his shoulder and every now and then he would stomp for about twenty paces, do a right about face, click his heels and return to his cage. A very attractive Grenadier and perfectly disciplined.

The golf course was rarely used but well groomed, except for the rough, where where was a growth of timothy hay which stood about two feet high. One would be lucky if the ball went into that hazard to even find it. I was constantly going to the sport shop at Windsor to purchase more balls. The Dean's nephew, Simon, became a good pal and climbing buddy of mine. He was a Grenadier and sometimes came to Windsor to play golf. One day he brought a young fellow of Chinese and Welsh descent with him. This man was the only person I ever played with who could consistently retrieve balls out of the timothy. He was an engineer. Whenever we would hit a bad shot he would drop to his knees, cross his arms to track the angle of the shot, and walk to the ball every time.

Alone on the Matterhorn

THAT SUMMER, AFTER SPENDING SIX WEEKS WITH THE DEAN, I decided to go to Zermatt, Switzerland and climb the Matterhorn.

I took a train to South Hampton, sailed to Antwerp, Belgium, then boarded a train to Brussels where they celebrated the World's Fair. While there I saw television for the first time. I recall watching an Italian tenor sing Schubert's Serenade from inside a studio, then leaving the studio to go to a nearby room where I could watch the same man on TV.

The Belgians were friendly but none of them could speak English. I managed to get by using sign language and showing them my train tickets. A group of them got a great kick out of trying to steer me to a bus that would take me to the train depot.

I decided to go down the Rhine, through Heidelbeg and on to Frankfurt, Germany on the Maine River. I had not seen or heard English-speaking people for three days, so I was excited when, as I boarded the train in Brussels, I heard a man bid his wife good-bye in English. As he came onto the train I greeted him and found that he was fluent in my language. His name was George Durr, he was Hungarian born, educated in France and Italy, married to a Belgian and had his business in Germany. George was a delight. He offered commentary on all of the places we passed enroute through Heidelberg and finally, Frankfurt.

We went into the dining car for dinner. He said he had eaten so did not order anything. I selected baked ham with all the trimmings. There were more slices of ham than I could manage, some leftover vegetables and cookies. Not wanting to waste food, he said, "Do you mind if I take with me what you have not eaten?"

I said, "Please do."

After arriving in Frankfurt, George took me to a reasonably priced hotel, Kolner-Hof, and then on a tour of the city. We saw the statue of Gutenberg, the man who invented the printing press, the city's outdoor theater and the Town Square where Kaiser Wilhelm and other kings had been crowned. The stone stage and bleachers there had been used 500 years before. The town hall and adjacent buildings formed a staircase, an inverted "V" design, which I took a photo of. Later, after developing the film, I noticed in the photograph a uniformed soldier with a swastika on his arm. That was the first time I had observed anything relating to Hitler's Nazis.

The next morning, when I checked out of my hotel, the hotel-keeper gave me a little note which stated that Jews were not allowed in that facility. That was the first time I noted any kind of discrimination in Germany.

Back on the train, continuing my journey to Switzerland, I got out in Basel to stretch my legs and saw a fraulein with a tray strapped on her. She had souvenirs, sweets, and I sighted a small bottle of schnapps. I said, "Fraulein, I am heading for the Matterhorn. If I am successful in climbing it, I will drink a toast to this mountain." I put the schnapps in my pack and returned to the train.

I spent that night in Zurich where I purchased an ice axe and some climbing boots with hobs, which were nails pounded into the center of the boot for the same purpose crampons are used today. The next day I took the train to Zermatt. When I stepped off the train, a Swiss guide greeted me and asked if I would be interested in climbing with him. I explained that I did not have the funds to hire him, thanked him, and then checked in at the Seiler Victoria Hotel. I walked around the village that evening. What an exciting place! There were no motor driven vehicles, only bicycles and horse driven carriages. That evening as I walked around the village, the Matterhorn loomed as the setting sun painted its summit. It looked much like the Grand Teton.

The next morning I walked the trail to the base of the mountain, fascinated by the mountaineer huts and other buildings along the way. The huts were ingeniously constructed. Most of them were two-level, with the barn on the ground and the living quarters above. This gave quick access to the animals, and the heat from their bodies helped to warm the upstairs. The beauty of the environment, the flowers, shrubs, and occasional rock borders accentuated it all. Some of the Swiss people I saw as I walked had accordions and they yodeled and sang as they came down the trail. I arrived at the Swiss Alpine Hut in the late afternoon and found there were no accommodations available.

The hut keeper suggested I get a room at the Belvedere Hotel next door. I registered there and went outside and looked through the telescope focused on the Matterhorn, an awesome golden arrow reaching for the sky. I ate supper at the hotel and asked the clerk to awaken me at 1 a.m. the following morning. That night I slept lightly, anticipating the knock at my door.

A line of climbers extended in front of me on the mountain that morning. Most of them carried lanterns or torches. As a line, we moved slowly and there was no way for me to courteously go around people. When the morning light came onto the mountain I heard someone yell, "Achtung!" The portly German just ahead of me ducked as a rock about the size of a watermelon fell off of the ridge above us. Had he not flinched, the rock would have taken his head along with it.

As daylight broke, we came to the Hornli Hut. I peeked through a window and saw a multitude of climbers still in their sleeping bags. The sides of the building seemed to reverberate with snores and guttural sounds from within. Soon after that the tempo of the people walking the trail diminished, and I was able to move to the front of the line. From that point on I was on

my own. I did not find the climbing difficult and was aided a number of times by large fixed ropes placed on some of the difficult pitches. I climbed at a steady pace and reached the summit before 9 a.m.

I had climbed the Hornli Ridge, managing to stay on the lee side pretty much out of the wind, which was really blowing when I reached the summit. I took my ice axe and dug a hole in the summit block. I was somewhat protected but terribly cold and decided to wait there until another party reached the top. While I waited I wrote a note in my diary: "I arrived here about an hour ago. The view is beautiful but I am too cold to enjoy it. There is a party below me. I hope they get here real soon. I want to get off this mountain pronto."

As I view that epistle now it looks like it might have been written by a fellow in his late eighties afflicted with the St. Vitus Dance: I was shaking from the cold. I wanted to traverse to the Italian summit but was afraid to. It was less than a hundred yards away. I noticed an iron cross that stood a short distance from their summit.

An hour after I first arrived, two Swiss climbers, David and Theodore Kroning, who were guiding a German girl, reached the summit. They were very friendly and I asked if I might take their picture, which I did, and they snapped one of me.

The Kroning brothers probably saved my life. They invited me to join them for a few pitches as we descended the upper part of the mountain. After tying in with them for about thirty minutes, I told them I felt safe and could manage the rest of the descent. I thanked them and took off, arriving at the Belvedere less than three hours later. There I collected my belongings and started down the trail to Zermatt.

About halfway down I came to a beautiful meadow and decided I would drink the toast I had promised the fraulein to the beautiful Matterhorn. I sketched in my journal the route I had climbed, placed my leather jacket on the grass next to the sketch, took the schnapps from my pack, laid out my lunch and raised the little bottle in a toast. At that altitude the schnapps took immediate effect. I was feeling no pain.

Just as I was starting my repast, I heard the sound of bells. I looked up and there was a small herd of Swiss cattle sauntering toward me. They seemed to be playing their own accompaniment as they came up. I had just eaten a few bites and one of the old bossies came over and stuck her nose in my knapsack. She seemed to want to join me for lunch. I have always thought cattle were strictly vegetarians and was surprised and amused, so I offered her a piece of cheese. She ate it and kept sniffing around. She ate bread, salami, and a couple of cookies, then started licking my ice axe. I thought, "What next?"

DAVID AND THEODORE KRONING, ON THE
SUMMIT OF THE MATTERHORN

THE BELVEDERE HOTEL, AND THE SWISS ALPINE HUT

When you're young you're a lot tougher than when you're older. All I had on was a University of Idaho pep band sweater and a light leather jacket. There I am on the summit of the Matterhorn, and just a beret, I didn't even have anything over my ears. It felt like the wind was blowing a hundred miles an hour.

—XM

Retrieving what was left of my lunch, I put it in my pack and started down the trail. The cattle followed me in single file, ringing their bells. Finally they stopped to eat some clover and I continued skipping down the trail to Zermatt.

I shall never forget that beautiful day on the Matterhorn, the Kroning brothers, the herd of cows and the lovely fraulein who sold me the schnapps at Basel.

Baron Exum

THROUGH MY GOOD FORTUNE spending several months at the Windsor Castle, I inherited the moniker "Baron" Exum, which in the future was the crux of a lot of entertainment, and later, embarrassment. It all came about through a series of letters written between myself and Gustav H. Koven of Jersey City.

Gus was an old climbing pal of mine who had let me stay in his penthouse during my road trip to New York to catch the ship to England. He was impressed by the invitation I had gotten from the Dean and thought it fitting that I should have a proper title in view of the fact that I was going to Windsor Castle. I became "Baron" Exum to Gus and his lovely wife Jane. I did not wish to be outdone by this gracious gesture so immediately gave Jane and Gus the titles of Lord and Lady Gustav H. Koven.

During our summer correspondence our titles were used freely, and when I returned to America, the fun really started. But first, despite my newly acquired title, I had to get through some tight spots on my way to meet Gus at the factory he owned.

Walking along the waterfront in Hoboken, New Jersey with my ice ax in hand (it was a pointed implement and I was not allowed to check it at the railway station where I had left the rest of my luggage), I suddenly encountered two ruffians who apparently disliked me because I was wearing a necktie. One of the roughnecks glanced at me, eyed my ice ax and with a shrug remarked, "Oh,

EXUM COLLECTION

JANE KOVEN, GLENN EXUM

■ *Jane Koven is Gus Koven's wife. She's the one we called Lady Koven and she was the first woman up the Middle Teton. Paul and I took the Koven Brothers up the Exum Ridge and then we did the Koven Route on Mt. Owen. That was the first ascent of the Koven Ridge on July 20, 1931, which we named for them 'cause they were with us. -XM*

da gold diggers of nineteen toity five, eh?" I gripped the handle of my ax and nodded. The other hoodlum cut in, "Oh let the damn fool go. He's one of dem goofy mountain climbers." I continued on without further problems.

After climbing the long row of steps leading to the Koven Factory, I came into Gus's office. He bounced to his feet, threw his arms around me and said, "Baron!"

I reflected his enthusiasm with, "Your Lordship." We laughed and had a good chat about my experiences abroad. Then out of the clear sky I asked, "Lord, why don't you come with me to Wyoming?"

I was completely bowled over when he replied, "Baron, I think I will. Just a minute." He went to his office phone and dialed his home. "Jane," he said, "Get the bags packed. We're going to Wyoming." I could hear her ladyship protest as she said, "But Gustav, what will we do with the children?" Gus suggested she contact their governess immediately and make arrangements for her to care for them. This Jane did and within the hour we were heading west. As Gus left the office, he instructed his secretary, "Wire five hundred dollars to our hotel in Pittsburgh." What a wonderful thing to be able to say. Then we were off. I in my open Chrysler and they in their La Salle convertible. As we covered the miles each stop encouraged more possibilities for the Lord, the Lady, and the Baron.

Upon arriving in Chicago, I left Gus and Jane to visit an old college chum who was attending the summer session at Northwestern, promising the two I would wire them at their hotel in Des Moines to tell them whether I would meet up with them again, or continue the journey by myself.

It turned out that I was able to get in a good visit with my friend and still catch the Kovens in Iowa. I sent their wire and addressed it: Lord and Lady Gustav H. Koven. Later when Gus and I were laughing about it over the telephone he remarked, "You know, after we received that wire our service improved 100%. They moved us into the bridal suite and asked if there was anything else we desired."

The next morning I saw the result of our titles as I rolled up to their hotel in my roadster. I was met by a footman, escorted to the lobby, and upon arriving noted that a receiving line had been set up to meet me. It included my good friends at the top of the line and the hotel brass intermingled within. I saw what was up so hurried to the front of the line, greeting constituents as I went, and arriving before the Lady as quickly as possible. I gave a quick click of my heels, bowed and graciously kissed her hand. We were all a success, and in the midst of great hilarity continued our journey to Wyoming.

Naturally, upon arriving in the Tetons, I concluded that our titles would be forgotten. Such was not my good fortune. That evening Gus and Jane went into Jackson for dinner. While dining at the Alpine Inn they came upon an old friend of Jane's from her childhood in San Francisco, who asked them to dine with her at her parent's ranch on the Snake River the following evening. Jane was very considerate of me and asked if I could join them.

The next evening I was petrified when they introduced me as Baron Exum from Scotland. I did not wish to let my friends down so I decided to play my roll to the hilt. I rolled my Rs and was in great form. My hostess inquired, "Baron, why do you come to Wyoming?"

I told her the truth, "I come to climb the mountain."

"What a wonderful compliment to our mountains," she chimed. We were getting along famously. Luckily, having toured Scotland quite completely with the Dean and Colonel Baillie, I was quite well versed in the countryside and the customs of the people.

All was going beautifully until the cook came out from the kitchen. Upon seeing me she ran across the room, threw her arms about me and said, "Glenn, when did you get back?" My hostess's face dropped and I lost my title much quicker than King Edward the Eighth did when he abdicated at St. Georges's Cathedral. That was the end of the Baron.

"Benighted" on the Eiger

I RETURNED TO ENGLAND in June, 1938 at the invitation of Hector Bolitho, the King's biographer whom I had befriended on my first trip to England to visit the Dean of Windsor four summers earlier.

I had also continued my friendship with Simon Baillie, the Dean's nephew, and had discussed with him my 1935 ascent of the Matterhorn. One day that summer he said, "Glenn, I would love to go to Switzerland and climb one of those Alps."

I said, "Let's do it!" We decided we'd climb the Eiger.

Simon arranged to get a leave, and on Monday, July 18, we left London's Victoria Station for New Haven, where we caught a ship across the English Channel. When we arrived in Paris, we stayed our first night in a little hotel on Budapest Street. Simon said it was a filthy little "dog hole," so the second night we stayed at the Hotel George V. In line with our move up in the world, we had a drink at La Reine Pedoghe in the rue Pefinniere, a charming restaurant made famous by Anatole Franc.

We left Paris at 9:30 the next morning. Because of the fact that I was traveling on a scant budget, Simon was a good sport and he traveled 3rd class with me. That night we took a double room, the only room available, at the Pension Dahiem in Interlaken. The room had a balcony and a magnificent view of the majestic Jungfrau mountain. She was beautiful and only a few miles away up the valley.

MR. WITTENBERGER, EXUM, AND HECTOR BOLITHO

The hotel was also primitive; one had to give about 24 hours notice before taking a bath. After supper we walked around the town. Interlaken, tucked away in a valley surrounded by towering mountains, was the most attractive place imaginable. There were wooden houses with window boxes and bright, colorful flowers.

By Wednesday, July 20, two days after leaving England, Simon and I went out and bought some things that we needed for climbing: ice axes, crampons, 120 feet of rope, and climbing boots. The boots were cheap but good quality. That afternoon we took a walk up the valley to the town of Lauterbrunnan to try to acclimate, get in shape, and find out something about the mountains and about possible routes. An old lady at the shop in Lauterbrunnan, who's brother was a guide, told us that the Jungfrau climb from the Rottental Hut was dangerous and should not be attempted without a guide. We had tea in the garden of the hotel and walked back to our pension.

SIMON BAILLIE, THE DEAN'S NEPHEW

That night after dinner we went to visit a man named Herr Schneider, who was president of the local Swiss Alpine Club. We sat with him and his wife on their balcony, and talked a while before joining the club, which cost about 40 francs each (the equivalent of two pounds). This membership allowed us to use their mountain huts and receive reduced railway fares.

Schneider was a great climber. He had lost two fingers from frostbite on one of his expeditions, after spending a stormy night in the mountains. Simon could converse with him in German. His wife, a homely, buxom woman with a nice, kind face, knew a few words of English and had been to London, so I talked with her. They were charming people. Herr Schneider invited us to join him the next day to go on a two day trip into the mountains with two of his friends. We gladly accepted.

By Saturday, July 23, after our brief mountain foray, bad weather moved in — thunder storms and high winds — and Simon and I had to delay our Eiger attempt. Finally, by Monday July 25, the weather settled and the Eiger stood like a pyramid reaching for the sky. We decided to attempt our climb. We bought provisions for two days and took the train up to the Eiger Glacier. The Eiger Glacier Hotel stood next to the station at the base of the Eiger. After our supper there, we went outside, had a look at the mountain, and determined that we would climb the West Ridge. It did not look to be too difficult, but we were wrong. Just as we made our decision, news came to the hotel telling us that Austrians and Germans had climbed the North Face, the most difficult climb in Europe, and had come down the night before.

The next day on the mountain I climbed with extreme care, belaying Simon over large snowfields at the beginning of our route. After that we were on solid rock for some time. Simon said he was relieved to have the help of the rope. We

INTERLAKKEN
DIVISION OF
SWISS ALPINE
CLUB --
MEMBERSHIP CARD

GLENN EXUM, SHORTLY BEFORE
REMOVING HIS CRAMPONS

had been climbing since 5 a.m. and by noon were nowhere near the summit. In fact, we couldn't see it at all and had come up some difficult pitches that it would have been unwise to go back down.

During the day we'd seen several avalanches. The sound of them is most eerie. Finally, at about 1 p.m., we could see the summit after climbing a steep snowfield. We knew that if we wanted to get off of the mountain before dark, we would have to climb more quickly. We saw the tracks of the Austrians and Germans as they had come off of the summit.

We stopped for a fast meal. Though we were not very hungry, we were terribly dehydrated. The sun reflected off the snow and burnt like blazes, as we sipped from a small thermos of tea, which was not nearly enough. Simon had a painful blister on his heel. He took his boot off, burned the blister and put a rough dressing on it. We had been wearing crampons because we had been intermittently on rock and then on hard snow. I told Simon we had to move faster as there was a storm blowing up and electricity in the air. We took our crampons off to gain more speed and put them in our packs. The storm was getting wild so I told Simon we were turning back and going straight down the ridge, that I would lower him down the full length of the rope and that he should slide if he needed to. I had him on a good belay and was anchored in.

After I lowered him, I instructed him to get into a comfortable position. The plan was for me to climb quickly down to the same place. There was a small rib of snow that I needed to cross before starting the descent. I stepped on the snow and found it to be covered with a sheet of blue ice. Away I went, plummeting through the air head over heels, bouncing down the mountain. As I fell, my entire life raced through my mind. I was not frightened and seemed to know that I was not going to get killed. I was wearing a heavy Italian felt hat which I had strapped under my chin. We did not have climbing helmets at that time, and I think that the hat saved my life.

I fell down 120 feet below Simon. As I came to the end of the rope, like a high diver looking for a landing, I pulled Simon off his perch. Simon landed just above the rock I had fallen to, on a flattened out section of the ridge. I dropped my ice ax and as I hit the end of the rope my hat came off and floated 5,000 feet down to the Eiger Glacier.

Just then I saw a rock which extended five feet above the ridge. I thought, "This is my only chance." I fell into the rock and knocked my left shoulder out of its socket. This felt minor compared to my right shoulder, which had been dislocated during the first part of my fall. I was in shock but not in too much pain. I had not injured my legs and, except for my shoulders, my body seemed intact. I got to my feet and called up to Simon to say I was okay. He was about 80 feet above me and in a very precarious position. The wind was blowing hard and a lightning storm was moving in. It was getting dark. I told Simon to be extremely careful and I would talk him down.

The first thing I wanted him to do once he made it safely to me, was to try to get my left shoulder back in joint. My right shoulder was too seriously damaged for Simon to help. So I told him to sit down, place his foot in the pit of my left arm, and pull. He did, and that shoulder slipped back into joint. Then I instructed him to drive in some pitons and tie us to the ridge.

I said, "Simon, we are stuck here for the night. I want you to climb down below us a few feet and retrieve my ice ax. [By the grace of God it had wedged there.] Now, tie us in and we must put on all of the clothing we have. We are going to sit here and hug each other to generate as much warmth as possible. I have a flashlight and as soon as it is pitch dark I am going to send distress signals to the Eiger Glacier Hotel."

At midnight I started signaling. An hour later we saw three torches moving across the glacier. By about 5 a.m., three Swiss guides reached us. They were surprised to find us alive, thinking we wouldn't have made it through the cold night. They gave us some food and some brandy, roped us up and we started down the mountain. My right shoulder was terribly swollen but otherwise I was okay. With the help of the guides, I climbed down without much difficulty.

Soon we were on the glacier. I must have been a sight. My hair was matted, the seat of my pants torn, and I was walking like a sidewinder. A group of children

THREE SWISS GUIDES WHO RESCUED GLENN AND SIMON.

came to the lower stretches of the glacier to see us. They seemed to be startled and amused. Later Simon said, "When those kids came up I felt like a bloody fool." I certainly didn't blame him and frankly, didn't mind entertaining the kiddies if that was what I was doing. We were very lucky indeed to have gotten out of that situation with our lives.

We went into the Eiger Glacier train station and I asked Simon if he would go to the stationmaster and see if there might be a doctor in that area. Simon conversed with him in German and the answer was "nein." There was, however, a veterinarian in the station. Simon had him come and look at me. The veterinarian did and said he would not touch me, but that we should go down to the next town and see a medical doctor.

We boarded the train and arrived at Wengen at 2 p.m. Simon took me to Dr. Oeticker's office. He gave me an anasthetic and told me to start counting. I said, "eins, zwei, drei, vier, funf...." and almost got to six before I was out. Simon said the doctor and two husky Swiss nurses got me down on the floor and wrestled my shoulder back into joint, which according to Simon sounded like a bone in a meat grinder.

During the time I was under the anasthetic, I had a dream. I thought I was in Chamonix, France, trying out to be a French guide. The head instructor was examining me and in the process felt the bicep of my right arm. That must have been when the shoulder slipped back into the socket. Dr. Oeticker strapped my right shoulder down, put it in a sling and told me to keep the sling on for ten days.

We went back to Interlaken and the next morning Simon departed for England. I stayed on for one more day before taking a train back to France and returning to America on a ship called the Normandy. As I look back at that adventure I feel badly to think I would have misjudged Simon and gotten him into such a predicament on the Eiger without having instructed him for several days and evaluating him carefully before taking him up the mountain. It is a magnificent mountain, but indeed the Eiger is an Ogre.

August 28, 1935

Glenn Exum, Pocatello boy, has just returned from an extended trip through Europe. He was the guest of Dr. Albert Baillie, the "Dean of Windsor," at Windsor Castle, England for six weeks. After an auto tour through Scotland, he visited Hector Bolitho, England's outstanding biographer, and Dr. Malcolm Sargent director of the London Philharmonic Orchestra. He met Prince Chavchavadze of Russia and Princess Gabrielle Ritbor of Austria while at Windsor.

■ The Dean decided he would like to take me on a tour of his homeland, Scotland. We traveled by train to Melrose where his brother, Colonel Baille, had a beautiful country home he called Harlyburn. The Colonel had served in the Boer War in South Africa. He was the father of my friend Simon, the grenadier guard who attempted to climb the Eiger with me. The Colonel also had a daughter named Fanny, and she went along on the trip. The plan was to make a circle of Scotland in the Colonel's Packard sedan. Fanny did the driving, I sat in the front seat, and the Dean and his brother sat in the back.

The first night we stayed in Calandar at the Calandar Hotel. They had a band and dancing. As the sun set, a highland bagpiper marched back and forth in his Scottish attire, playing until twilight. After he finished, I complimented him on his piping and told him that I wished I had taken his picture. He said, "Sir, that's no problem. I shall put on my kilts and play for you again in the morning." He did, and I took a number of photos.

-XM

This time we saw something fall out of the airplane. The object floated off the north face of the mountain and landed on a ledge about two hundred feet below us. I rigged up a rappel and descended to the ledge where the object had come to rest. It was a large silk handkerchief neatly tied to a beer can.

-XM

■ **IN 1946 PAUL AND I CAME BACK,** and we found so many people interested in climbing we thought we'd better start a climbing school. So that's when we started the Petzoldt-Exum School of American Mountaineering. Then Paul won a ranch in a raffle and had to leave and work on that, and I was running the concession pretty much by myself. He came back for a short time in 1954, and in 1955 I took the summer off and went climbing in the Canadian Rockies with Dick Pownall. From 1956 on I ran it myself.

■ **FOR A WHILE I JUST MOVED AROUND THE JENNY LAKE CAMPGROUND,** living in a pup tent. After I was married we were in the south end of the campground, when Ed was a baby, and we lived in an umbrella tent. Then the Park Service moved us up right next to the Crandall studio where we had a house tent. Bob and Fran Carmichael were there. Then we moved over to the CCC area—there used to be a complex of buildings where the climber's campground used to be, where the Vulgarians hung out. Eventually we ended up in the old CCC bath house. There were showers in there, and footbaths, and a big metal table we used to put our knapsacks on. That was where the CCCers used to pound their clothes to wash 'em. The floor had lots of drain holes.

■ **BETH AND I LIVED** in the north end of the bath house. I'd made up one of those Fibber McGee showers out of a lard can hung on a rope. I'd put a bucket of water in there and pull the thing up on a pulley, and you could lather up and take a shower, and the water would run under the stove into a drainhole. So you could wash the floor at the same time. It was really great. We had some of the happiest times there in the old CCC bath house.

EXUM COLLECTION

BETH AND GLENN EXUM

Beth's a surgical nurse. She came up to Kellog in 1938. She was working with the doctors in the clinic and I met her there, and we were married on November 28, 1939. She came to spend a weekend and ended up spending over 30 years there. —XM

I think there should be some mention of my mother. Try to envision from a mother's standpoint how difficult that must have been to try to keep house in a tent all summer. I think her cooking and cleaning and helping so tremendously with the schedule was a big part of the success. It was a big thing that Beth did. She was extremely proficient and supportive.

—Ed Exum

■ *We were always so confident of ol' Paul that we did unorthodox things. In the film, The Mountain, we were all descending the snow together, 'cause we knew if we fell Paul would catch us.*

■ *Paul and I would never drink water on a climb. We'd drink on the way back after climbing.*

-XM

54

GLENN, ON THE EAST FACE OF THOR PEAK

■ *I always climbed with gloves until the going got tough, and then no matter what the weather or conditions I took them off.*

-XM

July 29, 1932.
Fred D. Ayres, Irene Ayres, Glenn Exum. 10:15 a.m.
Grand Teton Summit Register

August 4, 1934.
Elizabeth Cowles, John H. Strong, Macauley Smith, Glenn Exum. Congratulations to Dr. Strong, age 67. He is the oldest man to set foot on the Grand. He climbed with above party in 5:40. He had the energy and enthusiasm of a young man.
Grand Teton Summit Register

July 6, 1936
Glenn Exum, Eddie Exum. Left camp at 11:25 pm (July 5) Arrived 4:13 a.m. Moonlight climb. Cloudy and short hail and rain showers. Visibility and temperature for climbing good. Waiting for sunrise. 4:43
Grand Teton Summit Register

July 22nd, 1936
Margaret Fulton Spencer, Glenn Exum. Miss Spencer is the first woman to climb Exum's South Ridge Route. She has excellent endurance. 5 hrs 45 min from cave to summit.
Grand Teton Summit Register

August 27, 1934
Geo. Eriksson, Fred Eriksson, Evelyn Runnette, Glenn Exum. Moonlight ascent. Cave 11:55 Summit 6:10 a.m. Fred Eriksson is the youngest person to have climbed the Grand, is but ten years old. He climbed with the disposition and gameness of an adult.

IRENE AYRES AND ALLAN CAMERON ON MT. TEEWINOT.

In 1932, Exum took Fred and Irene Ayres up the Grand in five hours flat. Allan Cameron was a park ranger.

■ *Whenever I hear someone make excuses for not being able to do something I think of this old Bannock Indian that tried to drive his car up a hill to a place we were staying. It wouldn't go up the incline, and finally he had to drive around the long way. When he finally got there he had the hood open and was watching the steam blow out of the radiator, and one of the hands asked him what was wrong with his car that it wouldn't get up the hill. His reply was, "Nothing wrong with car. Hill too steep!"*
—XM

PAUL WAS RESPONSIBLE FOR DEVELOPING THE CLIMBING SIGNALS. *I just kept fumbling around and experimenting with people, trying different techniques, trying to move people quickly in case of a storm. Some of the things were very unorthodox. There was one time in my guiding experience where I'd get up there and get around a friction pitch, and I got the clients all tied together about eight feet apart and started up. As they came up I'd just have them go around my back and I'd take the next guy, just like having six fish on a line. I could really move them, but technically it wasn't very good.*

-XM

GLENN EXUM WITH A GROUP OF STUDENTS, 1960S

Herbert Hoover

BACK IN THE EARLY FORTIES, Herbert Hoover came to Wyoming on a short vacation. A dear friend of mine, Mrs. Laura Sherman Gray, had spent some time in Belgium with her husband, Prent, who had been assigned to assist Mr. Hoover with a food distribution program in Belgium during World War I. Mrs. Gray was anxious for me to meet this famous man and asked me to take him fly fishing.

Unfortunately, our schedules did not mesh, so it was not until the last day of Mr. Hoover's visit that I met him. Mrs. Gray had taken him to town so he could have work done on his car at the Ford Garage. She brought me to the garage and introduced me to our former president. The work had been completed on his car and he was standing at the counter in the office, waiting for his bill. The young man, who appeared to be about 21 years of age and at least of average intelligence, looked straight at Mr. Hoover and said, "What's your name."

Hoover replied, "Herbert Hoover."

The young man looked at him and said, "Spell it."

Hoover replied, "H-e-r-b-e-r-t H-o-o-v-e-r."

The young man completed the bill and handed it to Hoover, never knowing that he was talking to one of our ex-presidents. Hoover carried off the incident like any common American.

> ■ *I've been in tight places where I said, "I can't do this, it's impossible." Then something inside me says, "yes, you can." Whenever it would get bad I'd whistle "Carry me Back to Old Virginny," and the next thing I'd know I'd be over it.*
>
> *—XM*

GLENN EXUM, PAUL PETZOLDT, AND JACK DURRANCE

Ed, Fred, and the Darkness on Teewinot

I HAD NEVER CLIMBED TEEWINOT, but had figured out the route to the summit, which was obvious from the valley floor. Two climbing clients, Ed and Fred, wished to do the climb. Ed was from Ireland and Fred was from France. They had been friends for many years and had come together to the Tetons. They were staying with Phil and Dot Smith at the LePage place along the Snake River.

We reached the summit of Teewinot at about 4 p.m., just as the peaks of the mountain were casting their shadows across the floor of the valley. We spent a short time observing the view and then started our descent. All went well, until we were about halfway down the face of the climb. At that point, Fred slipped. He slid fifteen feet, then landed squarely on Ed, who was anchored to a belay point. Fred was a large fellow and Ed was small. Ed freed himself from beneath Fred, ran down the mountain about fifty feet, and fell down.

I was afraid that he had been seriously injured. I hurried to him and checked him completely. He dropped his trousers to show us the injury that had befallen him. On his right buttock, there was a large strawberry, but otherwise there were no injuries. Ed staggered to his feet and Fred, with a Frenchman's compassion, embraced him and said, "Ed, you have saved my life! How can I ever repay you?"

We got our ropes straightened out and continued our downclimbing. Our progress was extremely slow, for Fred was hugging every rock, moving at a snail's pace. Finally, we were overtaken by darkness. By this time, we were on the grassy ledges and high timber. It was so dark that I could not see my climbers. I had them hold onto the rope and stay close behind me. We came to a place where I realized we were in a steep, densely wooded area. I reached out and found that I had stepped into the top of a pine tree. Fred pulled me back and we went a bit to the right and were able to continue through the darkness.

At about 2 a.m., we reached the flat valley floor. At that point Fred fell to his knees, kissed the ground and said, "Boy, you're sure 'dere."

They both complimented me on how well I knew the mountain. Little did they know that I had never been there before. I felt just as Fred did, and wished that I could have joined him in his affection for the good earth.

I Claim Thee for Spain

EARLY IN THE FIFTIES, I guided a group of enthusiastic young fellows up the Grand Teton. The group was elated over their adventure. One of them climbed to the summit, placed his foot on the highest rock, and, with an outstretched hand, exclaimed, "I claim thee for Spain."

My Only Accident

Several clients and I were scheduled to climb Mt. Owen. The approach went smoothly until we encountered the first steep pitch above Amphitheater Lake. At this point, one of my climbers, a doctor from Denver, slipped and his upper plate fell out of his mouth. We were desperate, for there seemed to be no way we could repair the plate, which had broken into two pieces as it crashed into the rocks below us.

We tried wiring it without success. We tried using chewing gum as an adhesive, but it would not stick. The doctor was almost helpless. He seemed to lose his sense of equilibrium and was uneasy and could not move on the rock. I decided the only safe thing to do was to take him back to the trail and get him off the mountain. He was fine on the trail, but completely helpless on the rocks without his upper plate.

"Exum just has an uncanny way of making you feel important—the man is just bigger than the mountain, that's the best way to put it."

—Dick Pownall

Glenn Exum   Dick Pownall

■ *We didn't guide the North Face and the North Ridge. We just climbed those mostly as something to do.   -XM*

DICK POWNALL   HERB CONN   JAN CONN   GLENN EXUM
AFTER CLIMBING THE NORTH FACE OF THE GRAND

■ *I think you'll be fulfilled and our hope is that the experience is everything you hoped it might be, and even more. It may take you a few days to assimilate this experience. We wish you well and when you're up there just sort of play a game of safety and handling the rope and in giving the signals. Give the signals loud and clear so your guide can hear you. Just watch these two climbers and see if you can emulate every step that they take, and in doing that you will feel that you are as great a climber as they are. Have a happy time.*

—XM addressing his clients

Bear Trouble

Two young climbers were camped in the area of the Platforms in Garnet Canyon. They went out to climb Nez Perce Peak one morning, and upon returning found that a black bear had visited their tent during their absence. The bear had eaten most of their food and ripped their sleeping bags. Their campsite was a mess. The climbers patched things up as well as they could and decided to stay on and climb some more of the routes.

That evening the bear returned and kept them up most of the night. Toward morning, they finally treed the bear in an alpine fir. They were so angry they tried to cut the tree down with their ice axes. Of course, this did not work, so they decided to move their camp to the Lower Saddle of the Grand Teton. They were convinced that the old bruin would not follow them to that area, which is at 11,500 feet. Such was not the case.

No sooner had they established their camp than the furry one appeared. The climbers were distraught. They stayed the night, and after much disturbance, left the following morning. They hiked to the headwall and descended the steep snowfield adjacent to the talus slope that extends to the base of the headwall. As they reached the flat area they glanced up and were amazed to see the pest following them, sliding down the steep slope. The climbers decided that they would turn that entire vicinity over to the bear, and returned to Jenny Lake.

I was guiding a party up the Grand Teton the following day, and when we arrived at our campsite at the Lower Saddle, we found that the old bruin had gotten into our equipment, which was suspended from a large boulder on the west side of the ridge. He had torn open the large canvas from one end to the other and had riddled our sleeping bags. There were feathers everywhere. We certainly could understand why the young climbers had been so disturbed about the bear. Fortunately, the bear did not return to the Saddle, but spent most of the summer in the vicinity of the Platforms, bringing excitement and misery to those who had chosen that location as their base camp.

Rattlesnakes and Carmen, the Barefoot Climber

PABLO AND CARMEN RUTHLING, 1946

During the summer of 1946 we met a very unusual man from Scottsdale, Arizona, who dealt in Navajo rugs and jewelry. His name was Pablo Ruthling. He was a distinguished looking gentleman — big and in superb physical condition. Pablo had thick, white hair, a bronzed complexion, a full white moustache, and usually went barefoot. He had a young daughter, Carmen, who was about thirteen. She was an attractive girl with a constant smile that displayed her even, white teeth. She had been born with only one hand; her right arm was rounded at the wrist. She loved being outside.

Pablo drove a stationwagon of an early vintage and always traveled at high speeds. His old car looked as though it would disintegrate at every turn, but miraculously held together. He spoke English and was fluent in Spanish. He had spent many years in Mexico and had a stormy marriage to a Mexican lady, which eventually ended in divorce. Pablo had great affection for nature and would begin each day by taking a plunge into one of our alpine lakes. He was a herpetologist and a collector of snakes.

One day Pablo came into our headquarters with his daughter and said, "I have something I want to show you." He went to his car and returned with a partially filled burlap sack, which he emptied onto our dining room table. We were horrified to see at least ten rattlesnakes intertwined in a great ball. As they unwound, each sought a spot on the table, tongues protruding and tails rattling.

Beth and I are both deathly afraid of snakes, especially rattlers. We were ready to go into orbit. Pablo sensed our panic and said, "They won't hurt you." He took a forked stick and held the head of one of the larger snakes, reached down and took hold of it with his thumb and index finger. He held the wriggling reptile away from his body, turned to Carmen and said, "Bring me the tweezers."

Carmen ran to the car and returned with a pair of silver plated tweezers. Pablo instructed her, "Now, show them how to defang a rattler." Little Carmen, with the dexterity of a surgeon, reached into the rattler's mouth and removed the fangs with two graceful movements. "There is no problem now," said the herpetologist.

There really wasn't, for by that time I had run out of the headquarters and halfway across the bridge over Cottonwood Creek to safer ground. Beth called me back and Pablo continued his dissertation on his rattling friends. He really had great affection for his snakes. He would fondle them and stoke them with the tenderness usually reserved for babies and kittens. We were impressed by his compassion for his pets, but felt much safer when he returned them to their sack and placed them in the car.

Pablo was interested in mountain climbing. He was short of cash and asked if I would mind taking my fees in silver articles. His merchandise was of the highest quality, so I was happy to accommodate him. He attended our basic and

EXUM AND BAREFOOT CARMEN ON THE SUMMIT OF THE GRAND

63

intermediate schools and decided to return in a few years when Carmen was old enough to climb the Grand Teton. Pablo returned to Wyoming most every summer for the next seven years. On the eighth year, Carmen came with him, ready for their big climb. We took Carmen through our schools, and Pablo joined her in the intermediate class. They both qualified with high marks to do the climb of their dreams.

A few days later, we drove across Lupine Meadows and started the trek up the switchbacks to Garnet Canyon. We had not gone very far when I looked back to check my climbers. All were coming along in good shape but I noticed that Carmen had taken her boots off, tied the laces together, and hung them around her neck. I inquired, "What's the matter, Carmen, do your boots hurt you?"

She replied, "No, I just don't like wearing shoes."

I put her boots in my pack and we continued. I said, "Tell me whenever you wish to have your boots, Carmen."

"I will," said she. Carmen climbed barefoot all the way up to the Lower Saddle. That evening, when it grew colder, she put her boots on as we sat around the camp preparing our dinner.

The next morning we were up at 3 a.m. to begin our ascent. Carmen's boots were in my pack. Both she and her father climbed like veterans, and we reached the summit six hours later. As we stepped onto the highest rock, I shook her hand and offered her her boots. She put them on to take the chill off her feet, but took them off before we started the descent. When we got to the overhanging rappel, which took us to the Upper Saddle, the one-handed Carmen was in great form and did the rappel barefoot and without the use of a guiding hand. Instead, she placed her right arm on the rope in front of her body to guide the rope, and did the braking with her good left hand. Carmen continued the entire trek down the mountain without her shoes. We arrived at our headquarters right on schedule. There were no blisters or marks of any kind on her feet or anywhere on her body. Carmen had been an inspiration to us all and has become a true legend in the Tetons.

DICK POWNALL, GLENN EXUM, AND MIKE BREWER

■ *Dick Pownall, Mike Brewer, and I were the entire guiding staff. Basic school was four dollars and a trip up the Grand was $19.*

-XM

■ *I actually only had two jobs in my life. I was supervisor of music in Idaho for 37 years, then of course I was in the mountain guide service from 1931 to 1978.*

-XM

The Rosegrower and the Piper Cub

A NUMBER OF YEARS AGO I decided to take my wife Beth up the Exum Ridge of the Grand Teton. She had climbed the mountain by the Owen Route, but we thought it would be a good for her to do the Exum Route. She was assisting me in the office and having that experience would make it meaningful and pleasant for her when she talked with people interested in doing that particular climb.

Beth joined a party composed of Dick Pownall's cousin Herb Pownall, a young photographer who worked at the Crandall Studios at Jenny Lake, and Skip Meyer, a rosegrower from Philadelphia. Skip, an adventurous type, was a guest at the Bar BC Ranch. He'd been involved in all of the ranch's cowboy activities; he'd ridden bucking horses, roped calves, and even tried bulldogging a steer. I had instructed him at our basic and intermediate climbing schools and he had done very well. I was the fourth member and guide of the party.

We had a pleasant evening at our base camp on the Lower Saddle. We were up and away from the camp before daybreak the next morning, and had rounded the end of Wall Street, the key section of the ridge, just as the sun was rising. It was a beautiful day, and the climb went smoothly. We reached the summit at about 10 a.m. and were enjoying the view as we ate chocolate, nuts, oranges, and "alpine ice-cream," a mixture of snow and strawberry jam. Suddenly we were startled by a Piper Cub airplane approaching from the south.

At that time, the Piper wasn't supposed to fly higher than 11,000 feet, and this plane was flying at something over 14,000 feet. We watched the plane as it flew north, circled and came back across the summit. Just above us the pilot dipped the left wing of the craft and then continued south. He turned the plane around and flew over us again. This time, we saw something fall out of the plane. The object floated off the north face of the mountain and landed on a ledge about two hundred feet below us. I rigged up a rappel and descended to the ledge where the object had come to rest. It was a large silk handkerchief neatly tied to a beer can. A note addressed to Skip had been inserted inside a slit in the can. The note was in verse form and I recall the last two lines: "And Skip, remember this for all your your ills: Be sure to take these two nerve pills."

I wound the scarf around the beer can and climbed back to the summit. As my companions read the verse, "Be sure to take these two nerve pills," Skip reached for the pills and devoured them like a thirsty man who'd discovered a desert oasis.

By this time, the little plane had landed at the Jackson Hole Airport. We descended the mountain without further incident. That evening, Beth and I drove Skip to the Bar BC and when we arrived, the attorney who had flown the Piper Cub met us at the gate. "How did old Skip do on the climb?" he

BETH AND GLENN EXUM, SEATED, AND SKIP MEYER, STANDING

asked. His face flushed when we answered that he'd done quite well. "That's odd," the attorney said, "He usually has a seizure around two o'clock every afternoon."

Beth and I were startled, and she remarked, "Skip did have a wild look in his eye as he came around the end of Wall Street."

As we look back, we are grateful that the Piper Cub made it over the summit of the mountain and that the pills were in the can.

■ *One time Beth and I stopped for lunch in Spencer, Idaho at the little cafe, and when we were walking out it was pouring rain, and you know, I stopped to go to the men's room. Beth was putting on her rain hat that came down all the way over her head. And I came out of the men's room and walked outside behind Beth and saw her standing there looking at the rain, and I put my arm around her and said, "Honey, don't you think it's time you should go to the bathroom?" And she turned and looked at me and it wasn't Beth, it was a little old Mormon lady.*

-XM

GIBB SCOTT AND I THOUGHT IT WOULD BE FUN to compare old and new climbing equipment, so he went down to the museum and borrowed some of Billy Owen's old equipment and I got mine. I had a new Ford that year and Gibb had Dick Pownall's Model T, and we set up everything near Jenny Lake.

Gibb wanted to be a guide, but he quit after guiding Theodore Teepe on his ill-fated climb up the Grand in 1925. Teepe died on the descent, on the snowfield below what is now called Teepe's Pillar. Teepe had made the 13th ascent of the Grand Teton. Scott said after Teepe was killed — "I'll never go anywhere I can't go on a horse."

-XM

Shhhh —The Water Ouzels are Mating

Dr. Henry Kritzler came to climb with us early in the 1950s. He worked in an oceanarium in Florida, where he had a pet whale he called Herman. Henry went through our climbing schools and did a number of creditable ascents with us. He was a nature lover, and when he was outside, always brought along a camera and his binoculars.

One August afternoon I was going to fish the Snake River above the mouth of Cottonwood Creek. I invited Henry to go with me. It was a warm day and there were insect hatches in the air and on the surface of the water. The mosquitoes nibbled on us as we walked north along the west side of the river. Henry did not have on proper boots for wading.

We came to a shallow section of the river where one could wade east to a small island. I was wearing a pair of hobnailed boots and decided to cross over to the island. After arguing with Henry, I convinced him that he should get on my back and I would carry him across. I didn't want him to get wet. We reached the island without any problem. Henry had his binoculars and camera with him and said he would be very happy exploring.

Some of my favorite water was north of us, so I took off for the fish upstream. I continued for quite a distance, and the farther I went, the better the fishing became. The mosquitoes were hungry but I didn't care; I was filling my creel. In fact, I became so involved with fishing that I completely forgot I had left Henry at least a mile down the river. When I realized what I had done, I hurried back to him. The mosquitoes were buzzing all around Henry, but he didn't notice. He was completely absorbed with his photography, focusing his telephoto lens on a stump in the water about fifteen feet from the river bank. Henry glanced at me and said, "Shhhh — the water ouzels are mating."

Another day, Henry was visiting me at our headquarters. Paul Petzoldt, who instead of guiding was now raising alfalfa seed and running sheep in the Wind Rivers from his ranch in Pavilion, Wyoming, came in. He greeted me and said, "Ex, I'm looking for a sheepherder to tend my flocks in the Wind Rivers."

Henry jumped up and said, "I want the job."

Paul explained that it would be isolated and lonely. That didn't deter Henry, who responded with, "When can I start?"

He and Paul departed that evening. Henry had illusions of lolling in the beautiful meadows and writing children's stories, which would be titled, Adventures with Schatzie Herding Sheep in the Wind Rivers. The adventure turned out to be a nightmare. He was so involved chasing sheep that he had no time to put his pen to the paper. When Henry returned to Florida that fall, he was relieved to resume his work at the inland pool, where he found a new appreciation for Herman the whale.

Dr. Henry Kritzler & Schatzie

J.D. KIMMEL ON THE BELLYROLL,
GRAND TETON

■ **JD KIMMEL** climbed some with Paul before I knew either of them. He wasn't a climber, he was heavy, but he was all muscle. JD owned the store and service station at Jenny Lake, and Bill and Ann Novotny and Nell Roach ran it. JD was an oil man from Oklahoma. He owned the cabins at Jenny Lake, where the rangers cabins are now.

He was down in South America one year and when he got back he said, "I picked up some jungle drums...let's have some fun." He said, "I know the Morse code and I'll teach it to you." So he hung these drums on the rail fence...a high tone drum to the right and a low to the left and he said, "I'll send you a message Morse code," and he said, "You'll be able to hear it on top of the Grand."

Well, old JD he got out there and "Booom, bump, bump, boom, booom, bump!" And when I got down that night he said, "What did I say?" And I said, "You said the fishing was good down here today." And that's what he said. The Morse code worked.

I don't know why he liked me but he did, and we got along. One time he said, "Glenn, I own all of this land down here at Lupine Meadows. Why don't you buy some of it from me? I'll sell it to you for $2700." But I didn't have the money.

JD really liked moonshine whiskey. He always wore a forty-five Colt on his right side so he could draw it in a hurry. I don't know if he committed a crime in Oklahoma or not, but he was ready. JD had this big black car... a Lincoln or a Cadillac. I thought it was the biggest car I had ever seen...but I was young and hadn't been anywhere. Anyway, one day three kids came in to the store at Jenny Lake, and they had a hicky, which is a little thing about the size of a nickel and is on a string, and they put the hickey in the slot machine, and if they didn't win they pulled it out and put it in again until they finally got the jackpot.

After the kids were gone JD came into the store and said, "Which way did they go?" He jumped in his Cadillac and raced down the dirt road, and whistled the kids to the side of the road and put that forty-five right at one kid's head. He said, "You kids hand over those nickels." So they did. And he didn't shoot 'em.

■ **RAY GARNER AND SOME OTHERS** *were going up to Canada to climb a peak there named Brussels Peak, and decided they might use an expansion bolt. They wanted to test the bolt to see if it would hold, so they tried it in the boulder behind our concession building. They hooked it onto the front bumper of his car with a carabiner, backed up, and pulled the bumper off his car. He said, "I think it'll hold."*

-XM

■ **WE GOT UP THERE ON THE SECOND ASCENT OF THE NORTH FACE,** *Dr. Hans Kraus was leading this difficult pitch. It wasn't very long but it was taking a while, and when he finally got up I yelled, "What took you so long?" and he said, "You'll find out." And when I got up there into the chimney, we later called it Upside Down Chimney, and the reason it was so difficult was it was full of bat dung. You know, guano. It was really slippery, I slipped and slid and I said, "Doctor, now I know what you're talking about."*

-XM

Oskar and the Barbwire Fence

He came into our office, bronzed and a seasoned mountaineer from Austria. He wanted to climb the East Ridge of the Grand Teton. My wife, Beth, was watching the office at the time and was hesitant to book him on that climb. It is one of the longer routes on the Grand and requires tremendous stamina. Therefore, she told him that he would have to come back later that evening and check in with me. He came, and after conversing with him for a short time, I was convinced that he could do the climb. His name was Oskar Dorfmann. He completed the climb with great style and from that day on, he became one of our favorite people.

Oskar was a mechanical engineer who worked in New Jersey. He came to the Tetons almost every summer and enjoyed many of the climbs in our range. He was a character. He had humorously documented many of the climbs he had done in Europe. He drew caricatures, and completed several of me and our activities around the mountains. I use one of his portraits on my stationery.

One day I was going to the Snake River to do some dry fly fishing. Oskar asked if he might go with me. I was delighted to take him along, and fortunately that day there was a good hatch on the river and the fishing was better than usual. I had a pattern that was a perfect match and was catching fish with almost every cast. I would hook a fish, hand the rod to Oskar, and he would play the fish and haul it in. We ended up with our limit in a short time. We took the fish home and that evening Beth prepared a sumptuous fish fry. Just before Oskar departed that night he said, "Zee next time you go fishing, I would like to come along and bring my camera."

The following Tuesday I had some free time and planned another trip to the river with Oskar. Oskar showed up with his camera equipment. He had a telephoto lens that was much larger than the main body of the camera. He'd packed both pieces carefully inside his knapsack. As we walked to the river, Oskar said, "Vait a minute. I vant to show you the power of my telephoto lens." He took his camera from his pack, removed the lens, and sighted it toward the southwest ridge of the Grand. "Focus zee lens about halfway up the ridge and you will see zee climbers," he said. He handed the lens to me and I focused. There they were, three climbers, moving slowly on the crest of the ridge. It was rare that we are able to pick climbers out on the climbing portion of the ridge without a powerful pair of binoculars. I was impressed. He put his camera and lens back in the pack and we continued our trek to the river.

Oskar was fascinated by every plant, bird, and rock that we passed. We were walking slowly through a thick willow patch with a barbed wire fence running directly through it. I saw the fence and stopped. Before I could stop Oskar, he stumbled into the fence and fell forward. The weight of the pack caused him to lose his balance and he was suspended across the fence. I reached down, grasped him by the belt and lifted him off the fence. Fortunately he was not injured —

there were just a couple of tears in his trousers. We got him back on his feet and as he looked up he said, "Look! He has been vatching us!" I glanced across the small creek that was flowing just beyond the fence and there "he" stood — a full-grown moose. He looked as though he had actually enjoyed Oskar's encounter with the barbed wire fence.

We continued to the river and had another wonderful day of fishing. Oskar caught many fish on his own. We even got ahold of The Big One, which we always referred to as "Grandpa," but were unable to hold him.

Oskar went to Jackson the next day and bought himself a complete fishing outfit. He became an ardent fisherman and usually had his rod with him whenever he went on an outing. Before he left the valley that fall, Oskar presented me with a caricature of himself suspended on that fence, me lifting him upward, the butterflies, flowers, and a bee buzzing in the sunlight and of course, the moose, with his tongue out and eyes aglare, looking at us across the brook.

ART BY OSKAR DORFMAN

■ We're two country boys, both with the same sort of background, who met and immediately liked each other. Got together and developed the greatest climbing groups in the world. —Paul Petzoldt

1950S EXUM GUIDES: DICK POWNALL, BILL BYRD, GLENN EXUM, WILLI UNSOELD, BOB MERRIAM

WEARING HATS GLENN GOT IN AUSTRIA: PAUL PETZOLDT, DICK POWNALL, BOB MERRIAM, BILL BYRD AND GLENN EXUM

TESTING HUT BEFORE TAKING IT UP TO THE SADDLE

LOWELL RUDD LOADING PANELS

JIM SMITH HUT

THE JIM SMITH HUT

Lowell Rudd packed the Jim Smith hut to the platforms and then the guides carried it up the rest of the way on their backs.

The guides who were on the Grand that day said that from up on the mountain it looked like some strange thing from outer space. All they could see was this shiny, odd shaped thing snaking slowly up the trail.

Ed Exum, Al Read, Bob French, Barry Corbett, and Jake Breitenbach carried the panels. Jake fell on the Middle Teton Glacier and rode his panel down like a toboggan.

The hut was built in Detroit, designed by Jim Smith, shipped to Victor and trucked over to Jackson. Al Read was the first guide to use the hut. It stayed at the saddle for 33 years until the wind caught it and blew it all the way down to the Middle Teton Glacier.

-XM

I asked Dick how the dogs got up over the Headwall — it is an eighty foot pitch and a dog could not possibly climb it.

Dick responded, "Oh, I helped them a little bit."

CHAPTER FOUR

Two Dogs and Seventeen Boys Climb the Grand

IN THE SUMMER OF 1952, 17 boys from the Teton Valley Ranch qualified to climb the Grand Teton through my guide service. Dick Pownall, one of my senior guides, and I were to take them up. The morning we left on the climb, Dick came to me and said, "Glenn, I have a number of things to take care of in Jackson. Would you mind if I met you at base camp on the Lower Saddle of the Grand later this afternoon?"

There was no problem with that, so I took the boys and arrived at the Saddle by 4 p.m. In those days we had no hut to stay in, and had tried most every type of tent, including pup tents and even an umbrella tent which blew away shortly after we put it up. The wind on the Saddle seemed to blow in all four directions at the same time, and it was difficult to keep any kind of structure in an upright position for long.

We found, after much frustration and experimentation, that a large tarpaulin served us best. We would take a climbing rope and stretch it between two boulders about fifty feet apart, take the tarp and lay it on the ground between the boulders, then pull it under and back over the rope. After we had placed the sleeping bags in a neat row, we would put our clients in the bags, pull the tarp over the rope and stretch it tight over the clients, and then place rocks on the edges of the tarp. The guides would then slip in the sides of the tarp, resecuring the tarp with additional rocks. We were "snug as a bug in a rug," warm and out of the wind.

The boys and I had done all of this preparation and decided to go down to the big snowfield on the east side of the Saddle to fill our canteens with water and prepare the evening meal. We had just filled the last canteen when I glanced down at the Middle Teton glacial moraine. Dick was walking at a fast gait with two large black Labrador retrievers following him. In about 45 minutes he arrived at the tarp, the dogs closely behind him. I inquired, "Dick, where did you get the dogs?"

He responded, "They started following me on the lower stretches of the trail. I told them to go back. I even swore at them and finally threw rocks at them. They seemed to have an affection for me and kept right on coming, so here they are."

I asked Dick how the dogs got up over the headwall It is an eighty foot pitch and a dog could not possible climb it.

Dick responded, "Oh, I helped them a little bit."

In turn, I replied, "Oh."

We ate our evening meal and shortly after the sun set, decided to retire. We lined the boys from west to east in their sleeping bags, and then thought about the dogs. I said, "Dick, I understand that the body temperature of a dog is much higher than that of humans. How about sleeping with them? You pick one of the dogs and I will take the other one." Dick was in accord, so he took his dog to the west side of the tarp, threw back the flap, coaxed the dog under the flap and closed it. After sliding the rocks into place, we too were snug.

At 3:30 a.m., when our alarm went off, Dick and I took our dogs from under the tarp and fired up the Primus stoves. I was elated. "You know, Dick, that's the warmest, most comfortable night I have ever spent on the Saddle," I said.

"You're right, Glenn," Dick answered. "We shall call this the Two Dog Night."

We roused the boys, ate our breakfast, prepared our packs, and were about to leave when Dick asked, "What shall we do with the dogs?"

I said, "Dick, there's no way we can take them with us. There are some short sections of rope over there in the cache. Tie the dogs to a couple of those boulders. Keep them separated."

After Dick tied the dogs up, they immediately started to howl, bark, and jump like they had lost their marbles, so I said, "Turn them loose." Dick and I have never seen such tail-wagging and tongue-licking affection. The dogs were in ecstasy, running among the boys, who were murmuring with affection. The stars and moon were out as seventeen boys, two guides, and now two dogs started the trek up the mountain.

One hour later, we reached the point just above the Needle's Eye and the Belly Roll, almost to where the Owen and Exum Routes meet. I said, "Dick, you have graded all of these boys. Pick the eight best climbers and one of the dogs and head for Wall Street and the Exum Ridge. I'll take the other dog and the rest of the boys with me and climb the Owen Route."

Dick selected his eight boys and chose one of the dogs. But something wasn't right. After some thought, Dick and I decided that if we were going to climb with the canines, we needed to know their names. I said, "Let's call your dog Lord Mallory, after the English climber who said he climbed the mountain because it was there." Then I thought about my dog and added, "And since we are climbing the Owen Route, I shall call my dog Billy Owen after the man who first climbed the Grand Teton in 1898."

Dick took his boys and His Lordship and traversed over to Wall Street. My boys and Billy headed for the Upper Saddle. We saw Dick and his group silhouetted against the sky as they continued north on the Exum Ridge. Soon we were at the Upper Saddle and ready to rope up and get on to the route that was discovered by Billy Owen's party. The dog Billy hadn't had any problems to this point. I took him over the Bellyroll unaided. The boys all were carefully belayed across the Crawl. (These two leads were the crux points that opened the way to the summit in 1889).

The Crawl is a horizontal crack that extends about 35 feet across the west face of the mountain. It is truly amazing; it almost looks artificial. Climbers are required to get into the crack and "coon." Billy Owen called it the Cooning

Place, because one has to crawl like a raccoon to negotiate it. It is extremely exposed. A rock dropped from that point wouldn't hit anything for about 3,500 feet.

The Bellyroll is actually a flake attached to the west face, and to climb it one has to roll around the outside of the flake. We then came to a vertical chimney, which I knew Billy the dog couldn't climb. I made a little harness out of nylon streamers, put it on him, got a good hold of the harness, and actually threw him to a boulder protruding above my head. I chinned myself up to him, then belayed the boys one by one up to the double chimney immediately above us. Billy was composed and patient. I felt that he could climb the next few pitches, so took the harness off him.

We quickly ascended the double chimneys and traversed the Catwalk, which took us almost due south. From there we climbed up a number of short chimneys, and were soon on the summit. It was about 10 a.m., the start of a beautiful day; the sky was a robin egg blue and studded with cumulus clouds.

As we enjoyed the beautiful view, Dick and his party came up the ridge to join us. There was something peculiar extending above Dick's left shoulder. Closer inspection proved it to be Lord Mallory's nose. Dick had stuffed the dog into his knapsack. In a matter of a few minutes, he had his eight boys on the summit. I inquired, "What happened to your dog?"

Dick replied, "His Lordship just doesn't like to climb, so I have carried him most of the way."

We had the boys sign the summit register. Then I said, "Dick, what can we do about the dogs? We will have to leave some kind of a record of this unusual ascent."

Dick said, "I have some iodine in my pack." He quickly took a paper napkin out of his pack and doused it with iodine. We then took the right paw of each dog, pressed them into the napkin, and left two vivid pawprints on the summit register. Soon after we packed up our gear and started down the mountain, we found ourselves at the Pownall-Gilkey Rappel point. Dick and Art Gilkey had set up the rappel on the first direct ascent of the North Face of the Grand in August, 1949. Art lost his life on K2 in 1959.

The rappel station was the most direct route to the Upper Saddle, and cut out a series of traverses on the west face of the Owen route. The rappel is a spectacular one. It is 120 feet, the last 80 feet of it free — that is, the climber is suspended without touching the rock. We had the boys all lined up and ready to go down. After two rappelled, the dogs became very restless. I said, "Dick, we had better take the dogs down."

He and I emptied our two army packs, and put a dog in each. Dick tied the inside shoulder straps together, so the dogs were side-by-side, placed his arms through the outer straps of each pack, then got into a crouched position and lifted both dogs onto his back. He fastened the waist belts together in front of his belt buckle. He got on a double rope and tiptoed out to the edge of the overhang. As he disappeared over the brink, the dogs closed their eyes, noses pointed up, as if they were in ecstasy.

We soon had all of the boys and the dogs on the Upper Saddle and were ready for the descent. I said to the gang, "Let's see what kind of a route finder we have here." I turned Billy loose and he guided us all the way to the Lower Saddle without missing a turn. What a nose and memory for direction! We were all elated with our canine's super performance, and we continued back over the moraine, glaciers, and trails to our climbing school's headquarters at Jenny Lake.

When we arrived, my wife Beth couldn't believe her eyes as we walked into camp with seventeen boys and two dogs. During or climb, Beth had found out that the dogs belonged to John and Georgie Morgan, who were working on the Elbo Ranch on Cottonwood Creek. I told Beth, "I think these dogs should have a certificate of ascent."

She made one out for Lord Mallory and the other for Billy Owen. I delivered the dogs and the certificates to John and Georgie that evening. When I arrived at the Elbo I said, "John, we just completed an ascent of the Grand Teton with your dogs. Here are their certificates. You owe me $40." What fun!

"LORD" MALLORY AND "BILLY" OWEN (TWO LABRADOR RETRIEVERS) CLIMBED
THE GRAND TETON WITH EXUM AND POWNALL IN 1952

Plane Crash on Mt. Moran

A DC-3 PLANE CARRYING TWENTY-ONE PEOPLE crashed on Mt. Moran's Northeast Ridge at 11,500 feet in November of 1950. The fifteen adults, including two pilots, and seven children on board were killed instantly. The plane was the property of the New Tribes Mission and had started its flight from Los Angeles, enroute to South America.

There must have been some problem with the navigating devices, for according to the log, the pilots thought they were somewhere over Bozeman, Montana. People living in the northern part of Jackson Hole watched the plane circle into the cloud-covered Mt. Moran area before it crashed.

The Park Service contacted Paul Petzoldt, the founder of and guide for the Petzoldt-Exum Mountain Guide School, and Blake Vandewater, a park ranger, to climb to the crash site. Paul and Blake started their climb from the Moran Canyon ranger's cabin. There had been a heavy snowfall and the two slogged through powder snow four feet deep in some places before they reached the plane, which had crashed directly above Skillet Glacier. It had flown into a large boulder, hitting it dead center. The two motors ripped away from the ship and plummeted onto the glacier hundreds of feet below. The speedometer was stuck at 175 miles per hour.

The passenger's bodies and seats had been thrown from the plane and were strewn about the ridge. There were no survivors. The weather conditions were severe, so Paul and Blake, after surveying the situation carefully, descended and reported back to the superintendent. The wreck had occurred at an extremely precarious place and the snow conditions made it impossible to evacuate the bodies. After consulting with the victims' families, the Park Service decided to leave the bodies on the mountain.

In July of 1951, the park superintendent requested that I, along with Blake, climb to the site of the crash and survey the condition of the mountain, the plane, and the bodies, and decide when to return for a burial service. The families wanted the New Tribes Mission to hold the service for their loved ones who died in the crash.

From the beginning of our climb at the Moran ranger's cabin, Blake and I were able to see the tail of the plane through binoculars. We determined the line we wished to climb and reached the plane six hours later. It was early July, and there was still a great deal of snow and ice covering the craft and around the

DR. GARBER CONDUCTING THE MEMORIAL SERVICE

ridge. Bodies and body parts were strewn about. Some were frozen in the ice. We gathered all the fragmented parts that we could and placed them in a deep crack that extended across the ridge. We decided that it would at least be a month before the area would be free of ice, and, after hanging a red quilt onto the end of the plane, returned to the valley.

Plans were made to revisit the crash site on August 10. This time Blake and I were joined by Paul, climbing ranger Dick Emerson, several doctors, an aeronautic engineer, and a mission theologian, Dr. Ruskin Garber of Los Angeles, who came to conduct the services.

We crossed Jackson Lake, and camped at a point much closer to the Northeast Ridge than the Moran area. The following day we climbed to the site of the plane crash. We gathered all of the body parts and carefully placed them in the natural grave with the others. The fuselage of the plane was still intact and the quilt that we had hung on the tail of the ship, now badly faded, was waving in the breeze.

The doctors attempted to identify the bodies, and took a number of jawbones so that dental records could verify the deaths for insurance purposes. Dr. Garber knew that one of the pilots, whose body was frozen inside the crack on the mountain, had been carrying several hundred dollars in cash when he died. The pilot was a close friend of the doctor's and the family was badly in need of money. Petzoldt, Emerson, Vandewater and I tried in vain to get the body in a position so that we could extract the billfold. The doctor, not satisfied with our efforts, said, "Let me try." He crawled into the chasm and after a short time returned with the money.

Dr. Garber conducted a beautiful service for his good friends that afternoon. We all stood in silence with bowed heads as he quoted the scripture and bid adieu to those who would forever

Climbing for Life on the North Face of the Grand

In 1957, Life magazine sent photojournalist Howie Friedman to do a photoessay for them about climbing the North Face of the Grand Teton. Howie selected Dick Pownall, one of my senior guides who had led the first ascent of the direct North Face of the Grand Teton in 1948, Herb and Jan Conn, two climbers from the Needles in South Dakota, and me. I had climbed the second ascent of the North Face in 1946 with Paul and Bernice Petzoldt and Dr. Hans Kraus. The route was first climbed in 1936 by Paul and Eldon Petzoldt and Jack Durrance.

Howie had made elaborate plans for the expedition, including renting packhorses to carry our gear up to Amphitheater Lake, and hiring two porters to carry our gear after we left the lake the following day. The porters were young, strong, and excellent climbers; both proved themselves to be great mountaineers in later years. One porter was Barry Corbet, who I later hired as a guide. In 1963 Barry was among a group of Exum Mountain Guides who were selected for the American expedition to Mt. Everest. He's also one of the first to jump into the now-famous Corbet's Couloir at the Jackson Hole ski resort. The other porter was Yvon Chouinard, who from humble beginnings as a blacksmith, revolutionized climbing hardware and equipment and became world-renowned both as an ice climber and as the founder of the clothing company Patagonia.

EXUM COLLECTION HOWIE FRIEDMAN PHOTO

Our plan was to be gone for seven days, spending the first night at Amphitheater Lake at just over 10,000 feet, the second night on the upper section of the Middle Teton Glacier at 11,000 feet, and the following five nights in the Enclosure, at an elevation of 13,000 feet.

We were packing the horses in front of Exum Guide Service headquarters when we were interrupted by a visitor. My old friend Dr. Hans Kraus had just returned from climbing in Canada and did not look well. Upon seeing the horses and all the gear, Hans inquired, "Where are you going?"

I answered, "We are going to do a photo shoot on the North Face of the Grand, for Life. Why don't you come with us?"

He replied, "I would love to but I'm sick. I was climbing in the Bugaboos and came down with a terrible cold. I think I'm getting pneumonia."

I joked, "Hans, you're not really sick. Come along with us and we'll cure you."

Hans, with flushed cheeks, said, "OK, but if I die you'll be to blame." He added his gear to ours and we were on our way.

We arrived at Amphitheater Lake in good time, unpacked the horses and sent them back to Jenny Lake. The alpine flowers were in bloom, the water of the lake was an emerald hue, and the moon was full at night. The stars seemed so close that we could reach out and touch them.

The next morning we were up and ready to leave at about 8 o'clock. The morning light made it perfect to get a series of excellent pictures around the lake area, and we trekked to the rim overlooking the Grand Teton Glacier, taking a number of profile shots of Mt. Owen and of the upper portion of the North Face of the Grand. We packed our gear tightly and traversed over the moraine and onto the Grand Teton Glacier. We made our camp in the boulders just below the steep ice and snow on the route that bends to the southwest, and eventually to the bergschrund that hangs on the North Face. We spent the rest of that day taking pictures on the glacier, planning our attack on the route, and preparing for the next five days.

I only used three knots in climbing. I used the bowline, I used the butterfly, and then to tie two ropes together Paul and I always used the fisherman's knot.

-XM

GLENN EXUM ON THE BERGSCHRUND ABOVE THE GLACIER. DICK POWNALL IS BELAYING FROM BELOW.

The next morning we packed up our camp, which included sleeping bags and two mountain tents, and went over the details of getting the equipment to the Enclosure, a task which required traversing back over the moraine, cutting south over to the upper part of the Grand's Lower Saddle, and from there climbing north and slightly west.

Barry and Yvon climbed up to the Bergschrund with us. I made the first lead up the very steep snow on the face below where the rock begins. Dick came up second and he and I inspected the condition of the rock and decided it would not be necessary for us to carry our ice gear. We slid our axes, crampons, and ice pitons down the rope to Yvon and Barry. Hans and the Conns climbed to the rock and we were ready to go. Yvon and Barry took all of the gear with them and started for the Enclosure. We took a number of pictures on the lower pitches of the face and were making good time until we encountered the verglass, which is sheer ice, in an area just below the first ledge of the North Face.

I was leading and it was difficult. I carried on until my hands became cramped and I did not feel safe continuing any farther. Pownall was in tremendous shape, and he knew the route, so he took over. The conditions were terrible. Dick and I had certainly made a bad judgement call when we left our ice equipment on the glacier. We had planned climbing beyond the second ledge on the face and then traversing due south to the traditional Owen Route. From there it was just a few hundred yards to the Enclosure.

Darkness was setting in, Venus had made her appearance, a sprinkling of stars from the Big Dipper were visible, and the full moon began to illuminate. All of this with no wind was beautiful, but somewhat eerie. I was climbing second, belaying Dick, Jan climbed immediately behind me, Herb beneath her, then Hans, with Howie on the end of the rope. We climbed in darkness for about two hours and decided to take a short break. Pownall had found a ledge that was wide enough for all of us to relax on for a few minutes. Once Howie made it up to join us on the ledge, he said, "I don't like being all by myself down there on the end of the rope." I volunteered to take his place, switching Hans into my position and placing Howie below him.

Dick said, "It's getting to be almost midnight. We had better get going." We were roped at 50 foot intervals and at that distance Dick disappeared into the night.

Pretty soon we heard his shout, "On belay!" Hans answered and was climbing. I could see Dick nimbly picking his way as he climbed out of the shadows and into the moonlight. He was not 300 feet above me and the echoes of "O-o-o-n b-e-l-a-y" let me know how Howie

DICK POWNALL, GLENN EXUM

had felt when he was on the end of the rope. Dick reached an elevation even with the traverse to the Owen Route and shouted down, "This is where we cut over." Here again we congregated. It was 1 a.m.

The sky was studded with a million stars and Mt. Owen stood like a cathedral drenched in the lunar light. The mountain seemed to smile at us as we continued our journey into the sky. Dick led off into the shadows and had only gotten a few feet when he shouted, "Here it is!" It was a rope that Howie and Willie Unsoeld, another of my senior guides, who also was a member of the American Everest Expedition, had placed there for us. The rope was suspended over an area of sheer ice. Had the rope not been there, we would never have made it across two sections on the route called the Crawl and the Bellyroll, which led us to the Upper Saddle and quickly to the Enclosure.

We were elated. We crossed the Crawl and Pownall led to the flat area beyond Bellyroll. I was still on the end of the rope and Howie was climbing just in front of me. Hans was anchored in the crack that opens between the broken rock that is the Bellyroll. He was belaying Howie. Howie was wearing a climbing helmet, which covered his bald head. He had a secure hold on the top of the slab and decided to make a long, swinging step as he made the traverse. In doing so, his helmet fell down his back and was suspended by the chin strap. During the stress of this giant step he had taken, he split the rear end out of his trousers, and both his fanny and bald head reflected the moonlight. We all sent echoes of laughter that drifted to Valhalla Canyon 3,000 feet below us. We finally collected ourselves, Howie adjusted his helmet, and we assembled on the Upper Saddle.

Our tents, silhouetted against the face of the Enclosure, were about 300 feet above us. We quickly went to them, and without hesitation, to our sleeping bags which had been arranged for us by Barry and Yvon. Hans, Herb, and Jan went into the second tent, which was behind and slightly south of the first. Howie, Dick, and I went into the first.

We were dog tired, having climbed steadily for 22 hours. Ours was a two man tent and we three, each weighing slightly over 190 pounds, found it a bit cozy in there. In fact, it was so crowded that there was no room for my boots. I removed them, opened the flap at the end of the tent, and placed them outside. By this time, it was around 3 a.m. We were quickly asleep and I'm sure reverberations from our snoring could have started an avalanche had there been any loose rock near us.

At about 9 o'clock I awakened, opened the flap of the tent, and reached for my boots. I was amazed to find that Barry and Yvon had placed our tent on the edge of a vertical wall that fell into a gaping canyon below. I quickly recovered one of my boots, but could not see the other. I was fearful that the boot had dropped into the canyon, and was relieved to find it perched on a ledge just a few feet below the edge of the wall. I retrieved it, laced it onto my foot, and went about getting the others out of the tents and ready for the day's activities. We assembled our cameras and climbing gear, and traversed back onto the face.

Howie took the classic picture of Dick leading the Pendulum Pitch. This lead had been Dick's key to the first ascent of the direct North Face nine years before. We took many pictures that day and actually climbed to the

EXUM COLLECTION

GLENN EXUM

summit. The next day, we returned to the summit and took a series of photographs near the top of the Grand, including some beautiful shots on the Horse, which is on the first pitch of the Exum Ridge. This section is called the Horse because the guides had their clients straddle it and "ride" across it. It is an 80 foot pinnacle shaped like the top of an A-frame house.

On that day we did not ride across, but had fun running across it. This was one of the moves Unsoeld used to enjoy so much. He would delight his climbers as he flew across it, never touching his hands to the rock, much like the movements of a ballerina. We played around that area for about two hours and finally rested on the summit just as the sun's last rays were hitting us from the west.

I shall never forget Hans as he sat there, arms folded over his chest, with the most contented look I have ever seen on a person's face. He said, "You know, I have climbed mountains all over the world, and this is the first time I have sat on the summit of a mountain and haven't been in a hurry to get down." We were only 40 minutes away from our camp. Hans was in his glory.

Howie took a total of 3,600 pictures and was happy with the results. He came to Wyoming over the next two decades and did slide shows about this climb. We were extremely lucky to have perfect weather for the entire seven days. Never once did Howie have to wait because of bad light or a clouded sky.

DICK POWNALL ON THE PENDULUM PITCH

DICK POWNALL, HANS KRAUS, HERB CONN
AND HOWIE FRIEDMAN

I shall never forget Hans as he sat there, arms folded over his chest, with the most contented look I have ever seen on a person's face. He said, "You know, I have climbed mountains all over the world, and this is the first time I have sat on the summit of a mountain and haven't been in a hurry to get down." We were only 40 minutes away from our camp. Hans was in his glory.

Howie took a total of 3,600 pictures and was happy with the results. He came to Wyoming over the next two decades and did slide shows about this climb. We were extremely lucky to have perfect weather for the entire seven days. Never once did Howie have to wait because of bad light or a clouded sky.

■ *Howie Friedman had a PhD in philosophy from Edinborough. He was really talented. He wanted to camp out at Amphitheater Lake all summer and read his philosophy books, but he put them up in a tree and never took them down because he was having so much fun climbing mountains. He was married to a gal named Daisy, and they spoke French all the time. I couldn't understand what they were saying.*

■ *The Conns were better climbers than we were. They weren't supposed to be able to climb, they were spelunkers, but boy could they climb. I felt like I didn't know anything.*

■ *Dr. Hans Kraus became the father of sports medicine in the United States. He relied on strengthening and stretching exercises and common sense instead of surgery. He had many well known patients, including John F. Kennedy. He was one of the founders of the sport of rock climbing, and developed the most popular climbing areas in the eastern United States. He grew up climbing in the Dolomites in his native Italy, and he emigrated to the United States in 1938.*

-XM

Two days after we came down, Howie said to me, "Glenn, I would like to get some pictures of a guide in repose." He rented a couple of horses and he and I went to Lake Solitude, which is on the west side of the Tetons, and took some pictures. It rained all the way to the lake. Just as we arrived there, the sun broke through the clouds and gave us perfect light. I rigged up my fly casting equipment and was blessed with some of the best fishing I have ever experienced. I caught fish as we circled the lake. Just as we reached the outlet, it started to rain again and the sun disappeared.

■ *I've always thought it takes too much energy to argue and fight with people. And you only destroy yourself if you start belly-aching around.*

Yeah, you just do the opposite. If you are going to kick somebody in the face, instead of doing that, pat 'em on the back. There you go.

-XM

EXUM AT LAKE SOLITUDE AFTER NORTH FACE CLIMB

Gombu's Apple

Five of our guides, Dr. Willi Unsoeld, Dr. David Dingman, Dick Pownall, Barry Corbet, and Jake Breitenbach, were members of the first American Expedition to Mt. Everest in 1963, under the leadership of Norman G. Dyrenforth. Of that group, only Willi reached the summit. He and Dr. Tom Hornbein of Seattle were the first to climb the West Ridge of Mt. Everest.

After the climb, five sherpas including Nawang, came to the United States escorted by sociologist Dr. James Lester, who had been a member of the American Expedition. The group drove from New York City to Wyoming and then later on to Seattle. The plan was to climb the Grand and Mt. Rainier.

EXUM COLLECTION

NAWANG GOMBU OF THE HIMALAYAN MOUNTAINEERING INSTITUTE IN DARJEELING, INDIA

The men attended one day of our climbing school to acquaint themselves with the techniques we use for the Exum Ridge. They were a vigorous group, always smiling and appreciative of the environmental beauty around them.

The day we climbed to the summit of the Grand, Exum guides Barry Corbet, Al Read, Sterling Neal, and John Huidekoper were in our party. Jim Whittaker of Seattle and Nawang Gombu of the Himalayan Mountaineering Institute in Darjeeling, India, were the first to reach the summit climbing from the Owen-Spalding route. I was leading the rest of the group and we reached the summit without any mishaps. Once on top, I saw a beautiful, delicious-looking apple on the highest rock. It looked to me like that apple had been left there by someone who had arrived on the summit before we did. I, like all guides, love fresh fruit, especially when I'm climbing. I picked the apple up and took a healthy bite out of it.

Barry saw this and said, "Exum, you may die on the way down. That apple was a gift to Buddha from Gombu." Gombu had reached the summit before I did and placed the apple there as an offering.

Knowing he had not seen me take the bite, I turned that side of the apple to the east and said, "Gombu, may I take a picture of you and your apple?" He smiled and I took the picture. Little did he know that part of his gift to the Buddha had slid into darkness within me.

In Search of the Trail

IN THE EARLY 1950S WE STARTED THE TRADITION OF GUIDE'S DAY, where we all took a day off and went climbing, usually a new technical climb or a repetition of one of the climbs we had already established. In 1959 the guides included Willi Unsoeld, Barry Corbet, Al Read, Jake Breitenbach, Bob French, Ed Exum, Stirling Neal, and myself, and we decided to climb Baxter's Pinnacle.

As we were walking in the forest on the west side of Jenny Lake we found a discarded sign that said "No Trail." I suggested that we call our climb "In Search of the Trail." We took the sign with us. From there on we had a gay time, and started searching for the trail.

Unsoeld was hoisted to Corbet's shoulders. He peered to the west toward Cascade Canyon, cupped his hands to his mouth and screamed, "Where's the trail?"

An elderly lady riding horseback down the Cascade Canyon trail shouted back, "It's over here!"

WILLI UNSOELD POINTS OUT THE ELUSIVE TRAIL

Willi Unsoeld, Ed Exum, Jake Brietenbach, Al
Read, Glenn Exum, Bob French, Sterling Neal

Unsoeld bounded to the ground and the search continued. Ed climbed to the top of the highest lodgepole pine tree, peering in all directions for the trail. He climbed down and joined all the guides in a huddle, planning their next move. They all joined hands and went into the forest, searching. No luck. They thought it might be hidden behind a rock. They all dropped to their hands and knees and continued the search.

On Baxter's Pinnacle, Unsoeld was carrying the sign, and after having made a difficult lead, set the sign on a narrow ledge and glared at it. He continued that procedure two or three times.

Finally, we were near the last lead to the summit. Jake led and the others made a massed attack: Four different ropes to the top. The sign was handed back and forth and finally placed in an upright position near the tree on the summit. We sat in front of the sign and a picture was taken. We left the sign there and I believe it was finally taken down by the climbing rangers.

We rappelled off the top, and then Unsoeld decided he would demonstrate an overhand ascent back up the rappel ropes to the summit. He did, and on the way down "rode the bicycle" and yodeled all the way down. He pulled the ropes down and we returned to Guide's Wall. That evening Beth prepared a meal of filet mignon, tossed salad, corn-on-the-cob, and baked potatoes, with peach cobbler for desert...a happy time indeed.

EXUM COLLECTION

Dr. William F. "Willi" Unsoeld, 1927-1979,
HE DIED IN AN AVALANCHE ON MT. RAINIER.

■ *Unsoeld was probably one of the world's great knot tiers. He learned all the knots from sailors, and he knew so many knots, he even learned to tie one knot that he couldn't untie himself. I never did use a harness, but I agree with climbers using the mechanical things they use now. On my last climb I still used a bowline.*

-XM

Willi Unsoeld *was one of the world's most famous mountaineers, but he did have problems sometimes route finding. One time he was guiding on Mt. Owen. He didn't get back and he didn't get back, so I got a bunch of horses and went up to Surprise Lake. Willi had been out all night, and we didn't know if we were gonna have to call the rangers or the rescue squad or what. But here comes Willi, down the mountain, playing his mouth harp. He got us singing. He had been out all night. He didn't always remember where he'd been or how to get back. That was his only problem, but as a companion, everybody was really fond of Willi, especially on expeditions. He was one of the greatest. He had such a love for people.*

-XM

The 50th Anniversary Climb of the Exum Ridge of the Grand Teton

I WAS DUMFOUNDED WHEN I WAS DIAGNOSED with cancer of the prostate in November of 1977. I was operated on and spent 28 days in the Bishop Randall Hospital in Lander, Wyoming. My doctor, Ralph Hopkins, found that I had a fourth grade malignancy and needed major surgery to remove it. I was released from the hospital December 28, and my son Ed, my wife Beth, my daughter-in-law Darleen, and my daughter Glenda all escorted me back to our home at Moose, Wyoming.

That winter proved to be a violent one. Beth and I lived south of Moose, Wyoming in a place called Meadow Road. Our house was one and a half miles from the highway, down a road that was not plowed in the winter. We accessed our car only by snowcat and snowmobiles. Beth had also undergone major surgery in Lander for the removal of her left kidney. I wasn't much help that winter; it was difficult for me to lift, shovel, or help with transportation. Beth, in effect, was pretty much left to take care of the two of us.

After a couple of weeks I could get out on my cross country skis for exercise. At times, I would go as much as a mile, but it was very painful and tiring. We kept plugging away and managed to get through the winter, which was a frigid, snowy experience. My pain continued and I had a bleeding problem, so I went to my doctor in Jackson, Roland Fleck, an Austrian urologist who had practiced in North Dakota and spent time on the staff at the Mayo Clinic. After careful examination, Dr. Fleck found that I had cancer of the colon. He immediately scheduled me for surgery and I was operated on in the Jackson hospital in December of 1978, and returned to our home at Moose in time for Christmas.

The second surgery stopped the bleeding, and I recovered much faster than I had from the first operation. The colon cancer was only a grade two and much easier to remove.

Because I was feeling so well, I allowed myself to consider an idea I'd had in the back of my mind for some time. In celebration of my first ascent of the Exum Ridge on July 15, 1931, I had climbed the route on my 30th, 40th, and 45th anniversaries of that date. Now I had my eye on doing the 50th anniversary climb of the Grand on July 15, 1981. The spring of that year, I decided that I would try to get myself in condition; if I was going to climb it, I wanted to climb it in style, without assistance. Although I was in constant pain from the first operation, I seemed to be able to block it all out when I got moving.

As my strength and stamina returned, it became apparent to me that I might actually fulfill my dream to make the 50th anniversary climb. It also became apparent to many of my old friends and climbing buddies, who began signing on for the trip.

Jim Klobuchar, an old friend of mine and columnist with the *Minneapolis Star,* arranged to bring a camera crew with him from Twin Cities Public Television in Minneapolis-St. Paul, Minnesota. They were all young and full of fire.

Pete Williams, producer of K2 TV in Casper, Wyoming, also planned to bring a crew, including two of the world's finest climbing photographers, Peter Pilafian and Jeff Foott. I was somewhat concerned and a bit nervous having two different TV groups covering the climb, fearful that there might be hard feelings somewhere along the line. But Frankly, I have never been a part of any activity that went as smoothly as this one did. There was never a crossed rope or a crossed word — all harmony and smiles!

EVENTUALLY, THERE WAS QUITE AN ARMY OF US, including thirteen former and current Exum guides. Yvon Chouinard brought Cullen Frishman, the then 14-year-old son of Harry Frishman, an Exum Guide who had just lost his life in a fall off the North Face of the Middle Teton earlier that year. The rest of the list included my son, Ed Exum, who had guided with me in his college days in the late fifties and early sixties; Al Read, Rod Newcomb, Pete Lev, and Dean Moore, my four senior guides who are now owners of the Exum Guide Service, which they purchased from me in 1978; Herb Swedlund, Chuck Satterfield, and Don Mosman; two other father-son combinations, John Peterson, my old friend from Minneapolis and his son, Dr. David Peterson, and Monte Later and his son Jeff, from St. Anthony, Idaho; Superintendent Jack Stark, veteran ranger Doug McLaren, who was with me on the 40th and 45th anniversary climbs, and Bob Irvine, climbing ranger, all from Grand Teton National Park. Yvon also brought a Japanese friend of his, Noway Shasikita.

DURING THE TIME THAT I HAD BEEN TRAINING to do the climb, Peter Lev, one of the guides I'd sold the climbing school to in 1978, and I agreed that it would be prudent for just the two of us to go to the climbing school area across Jenny Lake and do a few technical things. We went through the initial pitches which are done in the basic school area. I had some trouble on the Bathtub Pitch, a section of rock similar to the friction pitch along the Exum Route. I had to rely on the rope at one point and did not feel too comfortable. Pete and I ate lunch and decided to go over and do the Open Book. This went smoothly and we rappelled down the face. Back at headquarters I said, "Pete, what do you think?"

He replied, "Let's go back and try it again tomorrow."

I said, "I think you're right, but I did not feel too comfortable in the boots I was wearing. I felt my feet moving within my shoes. Tomorrow I will put on another pair of socks and I hope I may do better."

The following day we returned to the area and as we reached the bottom of the first pitch Pete said, "I have a pair of Chouinard's rock climbing shoes I'd like you to try." Chouinard did a lot of research when designing this boot. He actually went into the Swiss Alps and got ahold of a chamois' foot, inspected it very carefully, and decided to try to make a boot that would have the same features that allow these alpine creatures to move on the rock with grace and dexterity.

I laced the boots to my feet, stepped onto the rock, and was amazed at the holding power and complete comfort of this footwear. I felt great and did all the pitches without any difficulty, including the Bathtub Pitch. After we finished the Open Book, I asked Pete again, "What do you think?"

"I think you're ready," he said, "Let's do it."

Klobuchar, Monte and Jeff Later, Pownall, John Petersen, Doug McLaren, Jack Stark, and the TV group from Minneapolis met me at Lupine Meadows at 6 a.m. on the 13th of July and started a leisurely trek to the Lower Saddle. The cameramen did a number of shots of us before we left the meadows and also took a good many pictures as we sauntered up the trail. Brownscombe Brown and

■ *It was such a perfect climb. There was never a bad word or a twisted rope.*

—XM

EXUM & POWNALL

101

Marian Moore were doing the trail shots. They were all young and in good condition, but I was concerned with the tempo at which they were moving. They were actually running to get to the vantage points they wished to be in as we came along the trail. I cautioned them to slow down and take more time.

We finally got into Garnet Canyon and stopped for a lunch break. Noting that one of the crew had become nauseated and did not feel well at all, I suggested that it would be too much for him to go on to the Saddle, so two of them returned to the valley. I talked with Marian and in a kidding way said, "Now Marian, if you want to go with us there is only one way you can do it. You must slow down. I want you to get right behind Dick Pownall and try to emulate his Everest pace." She did, and arrived at the Saddle in great shape.

One of the most important members of our club was Dr. Roland Fleck. He is a delightful man with charm and charisma. Dr. Fleck carried a pack of emergency equipment with him, including his stethoscope and blood pressure cuff.

We spent a leisurely day at the Lower Saddle, waiting for the other climbers to join us. Dick and Roland decided to climb the Underhill Ridge on July 14th; by coincidence, Dr. Underhill, Phil Smith, and Frank Truslow had climbed the first ascent of that ridge on the same date that I first did the Exum ridge. The rest of us climbed up to the base of the North Face of the Middle Teton and tried to locate the pack that Harry Frishman left there the day he fell to his death. We were unsuccessful.

That afternoon the others started arriving. "Brigger," or Bill Briggs, arrived just as the soup was hot and did some of his famous yodels for us before he went into the hut.

The next morning we were up at four and departed from the hut by 5 a.m. I was in the lead with thirty people behind me. We arrived at the end of Wall Street, a long ledge that runs east and west, which is the key to reaching the Exum Ridge, just before seven o'clock. Pete took his Chouinard boots out of his pack, I laced them on, and we were ready. I had very much wanted to lead the first pitch of the climb and the plan was to have Pete belay me on that lead. But before I started a very important thing happened.

On the 40th anniversary climb in 1971, we had stopped at the end of Wall Street and I asked Willi Unsoeld, "Willi, do you have a word for the Maker?" He gave a beautiful prayer which lifted us up and caused the climb to come off in complete harmony and enjoyment. On that day, I did the entire route alternating leads with Willi. When we got to the Horse, a variation which leads to the summit of the Grand Teton, Willi was in the lead and ran across the apex of the pitch, which resembles the back of a horse and is completely exposed. I could hardly believe the grace and dexterity with which Willi

executed the move. And with only one toe. (He'd lost the nine others during the Mt. Everest climb). Willi climbed with the grace of a ballerina.

About a week before the 50th anniversary climb, when John Peterson and I were doing a conditioning hike to Holly Lake, I asked him if he remembered that prayer, and if he would perform it in place of Willi, who had been killed two years earlier on Mt. Rainier. John replied, "Glenn, I shall be honored to."

So once again on Wall Street, we all removed our caps, bowed our heads, and John looked up at the heavens. As the golden rays of the morning sun covered his face, his resonant voice echoed into the chasms of the Grand Teton as he prayed, "Almighty Father, hear our prayer! Watch over and protect us, and if it be Thy will, grant us success as we celebrate a long-ago historic event in the life of Thy servant, Glenn; especially, we commemorate his life, his leadership, teachings, principles, and example which have have turned countless persons now scattered across your beautiful earth in the direction of goodness and strength. Watch over him, we pray, as this small group and countless others accord him the recognition, respect, honor, and love which he has so fully earned and so richly deserves. While your eye is on the sparrow, Lord, let it be on the eagle here with us today! And Lord, somewhere in Your glorious realm there labors a friend of ours, doubtless striving to improve the lot of angels as he strove to improve the lot of men here on earth. Free Willi, we pray, from his heavenly duties and let him roam with us today in the spirit as he would have, but for Thy will, in person. Each of us thanks you in his day's activities and to share the companionship of this special group of men. In Thy blessed name we pray. Amen."

SOMETHING HAPPENED TO ME at that moment and I felt that I had wings on my feet as I flowed across the end of Wall Street, passed the big boulder and reached the base of the ridge. I threw the rope across the big rock, placed myself into position and shouted to my son Ed, "On belay!"

The procession started. Ed came across and then belayed Pete. I was hopeful that I might feel up to leading the entire climb. After the wonderful experience I had on the first lead, I felt that I was ready and capable of doing it. If I felt up to the task I had conferred earlier with Al Read, who had acted as my chief guide for many years, to keep the fellows in somewhat of a maneuverable sequence and hopefully have each of my guides do at least one pitch with me. I wanted my son next to me until we reached the last pitch on the mountain and then I wanted Pownall and Fleck to do that one with me. As we looked up at the Golden Stair, the rock was golden and the sky was as blue as a robin's egg. I led the pitch, Ed came up and then Al completed the lead with us. We continued on to the Wind Tunnel and Don and Brigger were tied to me.

We then went to the area below the Friction Pitch and I was tied to Chuck Satterfield. I looked up to the west to the crest of the ridge and said, "This was one of Willi's favorite variations. I am going to attempt it."

I managed it okay. We came to the bottom of the Friction Pitch and I did the first lead tied to Herb, then continued on roped to Yvon. We swung up to the area below the Open Book and I was roped to Rod. When I got into the Book, I brought Dean up to me and completed that lead. We then continued to the Layback and on to the Chinup, which brought us back on top of the ridge, where I tied in to Jeff Foott.

We continued along the Hogback to the snowfield that borders the Horse. Here I roped myself to Dick Pownall and Dr. Fleck. It seemed that the higher we climbed, the better I felt. The boots were really working. Wings on my feet indeed! I brought Dick up to the crest of the ridge, he belayed Roland up to us,

THE 40TH ANNIVERSARY CLIMB, JULY 15, 1971, WAS WILLI UNSOELD'S LAST CLIMB WITH GLENN.

DOUG MCLAREN, HOWARD CHAPMAN, HERB SWEDLUND, JIM KLOBUCHAR, MONTE LATER, GLENN EXUM, JOHN PETERSEN, PETER LEV, BOB MERRIAM, DAVE DINGMAN, MIKE BREWER AND WILLI UNSOELD

I led across the Apex, Dick ran across it much like Willi used to do and then came Roland flashing his white, even teeth.

The cameras were all set on the summit, the fellows were all there and as we stepped on top, it was like having a place in heaven. We took off our ropes, the fellows assembled on the summit block and I was overcome when they presented me with a beautiful gold-plated Chouinard ice ax, a delicate sterling silver belt buckle with the engraving "Exum Ridge," and the number 50 in the center with a profile of the Tetons in the background, and a portrait of me burnt into wood combined with a sketch of the mountains.

When we returned to the Saddle, the fellows had run ahead and were waiting with champagne. Most of them had to take off to return to the valley shortly after we arrived at the hut, but John and I decided to spend a third night there and return to the valley the following morning. We did this with much pleasure. On our way down the next day we just poked along, stopped often, reminisced over the many wonderful things that had happened to us the day before and for years on end, cooled our feet in the streams, ate, and finally arrived at the Exum headquarters at about 2 p.m.

Most of my memories from my Teton years are good ones, but I do regret not making a climb with you. The desire was there but not the chance. However, through the years I did send scores of people to your school to learn basic climbing skills, and all spoke enthusiastically of you. Recalling how Woodring was "agin" his rangers doing any climbing, I marvel now that Phil Smith and I were able to play hooky as often as we did and manage some good climbs. All the later superintendents seem to have encouraged their rangers to climb and have taken pride in their skill.

— *Fritiof Fryxell, in a letter to Glenn Exum*

Tom Mangelsen

I still make a game out of work. Instead of thinking, what an awful job it is to dig a hole, however it may be, you want to think of how beautiful the hole's gonna be after you dig it. And every shovel you take out, you know, makes the hole more beautiful. It just depends on what you've got in your head. I had a brother-in-law who was a fireman on the railroad, and his name was T.O. And I said, "T.O., how can you stand to look at that fire all the time?" He says, "I don't look at it, I look through it."

-XM

AL READ:

He was a musician and a performer in the sense that he brought that into his schools and in his way of dealing with people.   For example, he wouldn't just say the signal for "on belay," he would act it out, he would sing it out. He would sort of prance around up there. He was very fit, a very large, very masculine presence, and he would go through all these manipulations and throw his voice, and it was very effective.

We didn't always agree with him, and he did some things that we thought were awfully old fashioned at the time, of course we were young and he was thirty years our senior. He did not expect us to do anything that he would not do. He had very high standards, both of conduct and climbing, for his guides. He was alway extremely fair, and again if you did get outta line he would get you right back in line. He was a charismatic figure and a born leader.

EXUM COLLECTION

GLENN POSES WITH A GROUP AFTER
CLIMBING THE GRAND

BILL BRIGGS:

Glenn took care of you and did what's best for you. He always took care of
people. So in a sense that quality enabled him to create this guide school and
help climbing become a profession.

His technical knowledge was always way behind times, and everybody wanted to
update him, bring him up to current times. But Glenn wanted to
hold to tradition, to keep all that heritage intact. Some of the best
values of the sport were those that were developed early on.

Guiding was not a profession, this was an avocation. It was a
wonderful, pioneering time.

The integrity of the individual was something highly prized by
him. He could pull these people together and make a wholeness
out of it, which was a wonderful endeavor of his. It was
intentional, but the impression was that it was always just by
chance. He understood the values and the problems, even though
he had no words to explain it. This is a rare quality.

Glenn created a greenhouse for the guides to grow in...he called it
a fraternity of guides.

What was so successful about Glenn was that he encouraged your
ethics, he supported your ethics. He brought you together so that
you could trust in yourself. The most valuable item that we have in
a civilization is ethics, the individual taking care of his own ethics,
and Glenn is overlooked in his contribution in that respect. He is
just simply overlooked. Its value overrides everything else.

GLENN EXUM IN FRONT OF
THE OFFICE, 1960S

Glenn couldn't pick a guide but he could sure make one.

You got the traditional guiding coming over from Europe, which is an awfully
cutthroat profession — a jealously guarded, complex, awkward situation. And
Glenn sets up an entirely different ethical foundation for the profession, and he
doesn't do it intentionally, it's just that he thought it should be that way. The
European system remains to this day that you control your client within an inch
of his life and that's how you make it safe. And Glenn maintained the notion
that the client should provide his own self determinism. It's the client that does
the climbing, not that we pull him up.

ED EXUM, AN EXUM CLIENT, BARRY CORBET,
ON START OF GUIDING A CLIMB OF NORTH FACE OF GRAND, 1961

I think the profession owes what integrity it's got to Glenn Exum.

I was taken up with the fact of my own growth, and I first attributed it to Willi's influence or to Pownall, or to Corbet, each of these people I was working with, and finally it began to dawn on me that all these people are working under Glenn, and Glenn was taking care of us.

—Bill Briggs

Pownall was going over to tell them where the body was, and he put all eight people roped to me, and said to take them over to the Owen Route and go up that way. And I says, "Sure, Jack," but I'd never been up the Owen Route. I'd been down it once, and had no idea how to recognize it from below. Pretty soon we were doing some fairly hard climbing, and it took me a year to realize where we had been...in the Great West Chimney, which was Durrance's hardest climb. Well, we just traversed back out and eventually Dick showed up, sort of looking down, wondering about it, but he was wonderfully calm about it. I'm sure he never told Glenn. This will be the first time Glenn's ever heard of it, but he'll appreciate it now.

There is one really important thing — the handshake. Glenn had a bonecruncher handshake. It was the only insensitive, impolite thing he ever did. He would—arrggghhh! And of course you shake hands before you go out even to beginning climbing school...and he shakes hands.

—Barry Corbet

BARRY CORBET

BILL BYRD:

Muffy was a real good sport but this damned bear would come up and take her refrigerator and tear it off the tent house, damn near tore the tent house down. Muffy would yell and I'd come over with a flashlight and run the bear off, and he'd be back again. And we got really tired of this, and we'd tell the park, and two weeks would go by and we'd go through this every night. Corbett was ready to be tied and Muffy was a nervous wreck. Well the park never showed up with a trap. So Corbet came over to me and said, "We've got to shoot that goddamned bear or I'm going to get a divorce."

So I went up to the Jenny Lake store and borrowed...the guy that ran the store had a gun, an old elephant gun with an octagonal barrel that had been used to hunt elephants in Africa. And he said, "Here, Byrd, take this goddamned thing down there. You can't miss." And he gave me five shells. So I shot the bear, and then Dingman and his buddy started to skin him out right there in the middle of the housing compound, interested in the anatomy. And we thought, you idiots, do what you want to but get rid of the bear before daylight because we're in trouble with the park. So the rest of us went to bed, and we didn't tell Exum a thing, and he didn't hear the shot.

GLENN'S VERSION:

We had a bear that was giving us lots of problems, and they were afraid of the bear. So, unbeknownst to me, Bill Byrd went over to the Jenny Lake Store where there was a gun they used to hunt elk. Byrd goes over and says "I want to borrow your rifle to shoot the bear."

Pownall had his station wagon, and he put Byrd up on top of the wagon. And there was this big tree that ran straight up beside Unsoeld's cabin, and this old bear comes up there and starts up the tree. And then Pownall, turns the lights on, and Byrd lets him have it. He shot him, and the bear fell down the tree, but it just wounded him and the bear took off through the brush.

There was a ranger there we called Sargeant York. He heard the shot, and god, he came over there throwing rocks. He said, "Something's going on over here." Nobody admitted anything, you know, but finally this guy, the ranger, came back the next morning and he had a canoe. He had everything in it but a pair of snowshoes, so they called him Ranger Sargeant York, from the far north. He had binoculars, and he went around the lake to see if he could see the bear.

Anyway, they got talking with this ranger, and he says, "You know, you shouldn't be shooting in the park." He said, "There's a cowboy down there and he hunts with a bow and arrow. His name is Dennis. And if that bear comes back you could get Dennis to come up, and it won't make any noise." The ranger thought that would be all right.

And sure enough, the bear came back, and the guides went down and got Dennis. And he came up and the old bear was clear up the tree. Dennis went "twang" right there and got him right in the heart, and he fell and practically took all the branches out, and it killed him deader than....

I didn't know anything about it. The next morning I went over and they had pulled the bear over in front of the Ortenburger's lean-to, and Dingman was living there, and they were out there skinning that damn bear. And I said, "What are you guys doin' here, anyway?"

They said, "We're gonna make some bear burger."

And I said, "Listen, you take that bear, put him in a hole over there, and I don't want to hear anything more about it."

But Dennis skinned the bear in the meantime, and he was having his picture taken with this bear hide on the fence down there near Laurel's place. And I said, oh man, they are gonna run me out of the park. We can't do this sort of stuff.

But anyway, we took the hide down and the Park Service finally found out about it. They never did come to me but they ended up firing the ranger who told the guys to shoot the bear. So they got out pretty easy. That's a true story.

I think I am more of a mountaineer than a climber.
-XM

RON PERLA, ED EXUM, HERB SWEDLUND, ROD NEWCOMB, RICH MEDRICH, DAVE DORNAN, DEAN MOORE, AL READ, BILL BRIGGS, PETE LEV & GLENN EXUM

■ You know, you can't mother them every step you take. We had one guy who was down there at the headquarters where we had a big log where people used to sit, and he stumbled over the log and broke his leg.

-XM

CHUCK PRATT:

I never paid much attention to it until I started working here. I knew Exum Guides. I knew there was a place called the Exum Guide Service. I knew where they were. And before I met him, I thought that's not something I want to have much to do with. It was a conflict for me to have close friends who were Exum guides. Until I met Glenn, and that just made all the difference.

Here was the gentleman of such grace and integrity, that my rule of guides as prostitutes just dissolved. Just disappeared.

DEAN MOORE:

He was the first on the bandwagon to actually come out and say to males, don't be afraid as a male to show love and care. You'll be happier if you respect and love each other.

DR. JOHN PETERSEN:

Glenn finds nothing more intriguing than to take someone who doesn't know anything about climbing and make him into a good climber.

On the 50th anniversary climb, back in 1981, he was seventy years old and I was 69, I noticed as he got higher, as the day wore on, he actually got better. He was climbing with more flair, with more certainty, with more assuredness near the summit than when we started. He seems to respond to the atmosphere of the mountain and the stimulation of the people he's with. When we got to the top of the mountain, he was seventy years old, climbing just beautifully, his balance and sense of rhythm were superb.

After we got back down to the Saddle, Glenn looked at me and said, "Ya know, I think we ought to stay here tonight." And we did. We had enough food and we came down the next day. We started at eight o'clock and we didn't get back down until almost four in the afternoon, so you know how much fun we had on the way down. We laughed and told stories. He is full of stories, and some I've

EXUM GUIDES, 1959

JAKE BREITENBACH, BOB FRENCH, AL READ, BARRY CORBET, ED EXUM, GLENN EXUM & WILLI UNSOELD

heard, and when he'd say, "Have I told you about....?" and he'd go on about some tale and I'd say, "Yes, you have." Well he'd say, "That's all right, it's a good story and I'd like to hear it again myself." And we'd hear it again.

We're both lousy golfers, and yet this is characteristic of Glenn, every time we go out he says, "Well now, today we're going to show them, aren't we?" His optimism never wavers.

He has long since said that he only made one mistake in choosing guides, he failed to choose Chouinard. Yvon walked in one day and you know how, if you know Yvon, how he can look. He can look like he just stepped out of the Salvation Army ragbag. He can look just like a little worn out bum, and I'd say that if he were sitting here he'd laugh about it.

HERB SWEDLUND:

Glenn always considered himself to be a very simple man. He wasn't simple by any means — he was very, very complex. He was one of the most intuitive people I've met, and he had a very excellent understanding of the human mind. He brought out the best in us.

Xm, Bill Briggs, Chuck Satterfield, Will Bassett, Dean Moore, Don Mosman, John Spar, Herb Swedlund, Jeff Foott, Rod Newcomb, Rod Dornan, R. Ream

Back: Dick Pownall, Doug McLaren, Jack Stark, Jim Klobuchar, Xm
Front: John Petersen, Monte Later, Pete Wiliams

He was much bigger than any of us, and when he wanted he would simply be able to pick you up and take you in the back room. When you walked into the guide service and Glenn said, "Herb, I would like to speak to you for a moment in the back room," it was very frightening.

Glenn was meticulous. He took care of everything. Used equipment was repaired, it was never thrown out. Sometimes we got very frustrated with that. Glenn was very frugal. When those ropes became quite old, well, very often Glenn would want to hang on to them 'cause they would certainly suffice. They were perfectly safe for basic school, but at the same time we were embarrassed by them 'cause they would look so frayed and shoddy and dirty. And people would say, "Do you actually use ropes like this to climb a mountain?" Sometimes we would have to take the ropes and hide them, or bury them, or, sometimes we would tie rocks to them, you can't say this, and throw them in Jenny Lake so we could get new ropes.

People looked up to him and they loved listening to him talk. He was a great talker, a marvelous talker. He liked to talk and give speeches, and that's what he did. Every day he would come out and it was like the principal of the school was here, directing the whole thing....he was conducting this whole orchestra and people absolutely loved it.

■ *I don't know why, but I felt I understood the guides. I admired their ability so much, each of them, and I knew they were all innately bright. They were just kind of floating around. But I used to always tell 'em, "Fellas, someday you are going to have to be a stable person."*

-XM

JOANNE BYRD:

I don't think I ever worried at all. I had a great deal of confidence in all the guides' ability. Glenn was marvelous, he was extremely concerned with the safety.

He is one of the most affirmative people that I've ever known in my life. I've never known anyone who appreciates life more, appreciates people more, is more encouraging.

XM &
DURRANCE

JACK DURRANCE:

He was a starry eyed-music teacher who saw only the best things in some of the worst rogues in the world, and he kept them together.

JEFF FOOTT:

When I was first thinking about becoming a wildlife photographer and getting into film, I was poking around trying to find animals, and at that time the only encouragement I got was from Glenn. My parents were against it and my friends thought it was a nice hobby, but Glenn was the only person to give me support.

Glenn had a nice rapport with all the guides. He especially took care of the bachelors, and Beth made sure they were invited over and had at least one good dinner a week.

On Guide's Day we would take the day off and have a festive gathering, and one person there who was very close to Glenn was Uncle Clarence. He was a sort of vaudeville actor and he would come and do his same routines every year, and every year they were just as funny. It was the one time Glenn relaxed. He and Clarence used to go out back and have a little drink of whiskey or whatever and then tell some stories about the old days. I think we got the best stories during those Guide Days when Uncle Clarence was around.

A lot of his traits he insisted on his guides following were useful later on, like being on time. He had a very strong attachment to punctuality.

Paul Petzoldt really took care of Glenn in those old days, taught him all about climbing and guiding. Glenn has still maintained his original fondness for him.

MIRIAM UNDERHILL:

Glenn is the only man to offer to lend me his pants. We were coming down that gully, trying to cut over to the regular route up by Amphitheater Lake, and it was all full of bushes and scratchy, and I had on shorts. So we met Glenn and he said, "Oh, this is terrible, I'll swap pants with you." He had on long blue jeans. "I'll swap pants with you."

MARGARET SMITH CRAIGHEAD:

They had a shoe last out in the campground, and all the climbers would hammer
in their own hobnails.

PAUL PETZOLDT:

I've always had a very strong emotional attachment for Glenn, and it might have
been because we had similar backgrounds. I came here as a homeless kid. He
was more of a brother to me than any of my brothers.

PETE LEV:

I think what Glenn did was to basically set the mechanism for a guide to make a
livelihood; not a livelihood for a summer college kid but for a grownup.
I was part of that era, kind of the Golden Age. It's one thing to go around the
world and do first ascents of peaks, but Glenn never did that. He stayed home

and took people up the Tetons. To many of the leading edge climbers this looks like a humble task, but there are certain virtues to humble tasks that I didn't appreciate when I was twenty. I think Glenn should be honored for steadfastly pursuing the humble task of taking folks up the Tetons. He showed us there is a lot of good reward there.

Glenn had very high ethical standards for himself, and he expected the same for his guides.

PETE SINCLAIR:

He was innovative in his time. No one else was doing what he did. No one else had a professional standard for guides.

He survived the 60's. Few authority figures survived. Glenn did.

ROD NEWCOMB:

Glenn's Uncle Clarence was also a gifted craftsman. One summer the guide shack just collapsed, and he rebuilt it. Up in the attic are all these posts......Glenn didn't want to waste good lumber on an old shack, so they cut posts out of the woods to reinforce the structure.
I'd show up in old climbing pants...the ones I remember were knickers, and they began to develop some holes. Glenn would say, "Rod, go down to Teton Mountaineering and buy a pair of trousers and charge them to me." So on the one hand he was fiscally tight and on the other he was generous. All in all he was just a great boss.

YVON CHOUINARD:

We were carrying loads to the Upper Saddle when Glenn was on the North Face. For $25 each Barry and I carried an entire horseload up to the Upper Saddle by way of the Black Dike. There was a massive amount of stuff. Barry did it in one trip, well over a hundred pounds. He couldn't get up..I had to help him stand up. I did two trips.

I still see him with his old porkpie hat on at a rakish angle.

YVON CHOUINARD IN EARLY HOUSING

Glenn was probably the best kind of leader 'cause he was always very fair, never excitable, so that no matter what happened he was always under control. He always had a lot of confidence in everybody.

Glenn used to go out and meet every client and introduce the guide, and he always made it sound as if they were going to get the world's best climber, so the clients would always put a lot of trust in the guide straight off, because people would really believe Glenn ...he had that authority about him.

Glenn took guiding very seriously. I think he had over 300 ascents of the Grand and only failed getting to the summit two or three times. The best guides fail now probably one out of ten or twenty times because of weather. Glenn would inspire a little more, and he had more leeway in being able to stay up an extra day if the weather was bad.

I know climbers who grew up without a strong father figure, and Glenn provided that for a lot of young guides and climbers. He was a perfect one for that..he was a perfect teacher. He was absolutely consistent...you knew exactly where Glenn stood. He wasn't inflexible, but he was very consistent.

■ *You know, Yvon wanted to guide for me. Yvon, when he was barefoot and long-haired and living in the incinerator. But I loved and always did love Yvon. But I was ashamed of his appearance. And I think as I look at his life and what he's done with it, that he is probably better off never having been an Exum guide.*

-XM

121

It took me twenty years to get over Dad selling the guiding school. I grew up watching Al Read, Dean Moore, Pete Lev, Bill Briggs, Rod Newcomb, all the guides. I always wanted to climb more but I didn't want to take advantage of the situation, being the owner's daughter. But Dad noticed and sent me up Cube Point with Jake Breitenbach, and he took me up the Grand when I was fourteen.

-Glenda Exum Faulk

GLENDA AND ED EXUM ON THE GRAND

GLENDA EXUM FAULK:

Dad taught me to be optimistic about everything. He is a gentleman and a gentle man — the greatest, most positive person I've ever met. Also the most forgiving — he loves everybody.

He even taught me in school, and gave me a real appreciation for music. When he conducted he never used a baton — just his big hands. I went to his retirement concert, and I remember crying when I saw the expression of pure joy on his face while he conducted.

He always said that how you keep yourself and your surroundings is a reflection of who you are. There were no weeds or trash in Dad's yard.

BACK ROW:
BARRY CORBET, BILL BYRD, PETE SINCLAIR, ED EXUM, RICK MEDRICK, HERB SWEDLUND,
BILL BRIGGS, PETE LEV, FRED WRIGHT, AL READ, RICK HORN, ROD NEWCOMB, PAUL PETZOLDT,
GLENN EXUM

FIRST ROW:
SHERPAS FROM THE 1963 EVEREST CLIMB

124

I WANT TO THANK MY FAMILY for their support while I wrote my stories and took the time away from them to work on this book. Especially my loving wife Beth. My daughter Glenda and my son Ed encouraged me also, and gave me the love and understanding I needed.

My old pal Yvon Chouinard got me started on this book years ago and never gave up trying to convince me to keep going. He is an amazing fellow.

My friend Tom Mangelsen is like another son to us. He is one of the best photographers in the world and a very talented guy.

Charlie Craighead created this book out of my notes and stories and old photographs. I don't know how he did it.

I want to mention my dear friends Jack and Margaret Huyler. I thank them for their friendship and love over the many years. And to the memory of Jack's brother, Colter.

Al Read, Rod Newcomb, Pete Lev, and Dean Moore bought the Exum guide concession from me and I am proud of them and the way they have run the business. I wish them many happy years guiding in the Tetons.
I have been blessed with countless memories of friends and places. To all the climbers no longer with us I want to send a special thanks for being able to share those moments in the mountains. Friends like Hans Kraus and Willi Unsoeld.

My old pals Dick Pownall and Paul Petzoldt are an inspiration to me.

To the loving memory of my brother Eddie, and to the memory of my parents.

God bless you all,

Glenn Exum

GLENN TOLD ME THAT WRITING AND PUBLISHING THIS BOOK involved more backtracking and delays than the worst climbing route he ever faced. But in true Exum fashion he smiled and sang the whole time.

I inherited this project from Jean Weiss. The big plastic tub of material she dragged in my front door one day on her way out of town was the basis of this book. She deserves the credit for patiently helping Glenn get his stories in shape, and for taking wonderful oral histories from Glenn's friends and peers. Some additional material came from Lorraine Bonney, who generously offered it to this end.

To use a corny climbing metaphor, Yvon Chouinard belayed this project from the beginning. And like a good belayer, he paid attention; every time we needed it, Yvon was there immediately with "more rope." He initially encouraged Glenn, and finally convinced him to sit down and write his stories. He made Glenn believe in himself and his story just as Glenn once inspired Yvon.

Tom Mangelsen was also there from the the first days to encourage Glenn, support the book, and act as a sounding board for the material. Tom freely gave photographs, film, scans, and the use of his home so Glenn could work with me. He also entertained Glenn with Loupe, the smartest dog in the world, and gave Glenn the love and moral support he needed to go on.

Al Read, Rod Newcomb, Peter Lev and the Exum Mountain Guides gave their complete support. They provided invaluable information about the guide service, names, dates, and events. They drove Glenn to meet with me and offered the climber's companionship he needed.

I was supported in my work by Yvon Chouinard, Tom Mangelsen, Glenn and Beth Exum, and Exum Mountain Guides. They all believed me when I said that "Glenn's book" was there, and we just had to find the pieces and put them together.

Photographs came from all over, but mostly from Glenn's collection. Some of the photographs were taken by climbers and friends long gone. We know they would want to be a part of this, and thank them. For some photos we never found out who was holding the camera. Dick Pownall has to be commended for his persistent search, finally coming up with the last known print of the two dogs on the summit of the Grand.

The warmest thanks to Glenn and Beth Exum, who graciously let me into their lives to do this, and who never questioned my direction.

And to Bill Swift and Jack Neckels, of Grand Teton National Park, who helped this book become a part of the local history. Bill somehow squeezed a few extra hours into his day to review the manuscript.

And Sharlene Milligan, Grand Teton Natural History Association, who pushed to have Glenn's book become a reality and give it a home in the Tetons.

This is Glenn's book. I think it reflects his gentlemanly nature, humor, and compassion.

-Charlie Craighead

128

Al Williamson (NPS climbing ranger), Julie Petersen (Fritiof Fryxell's niece), and Exum

Profits from this book will support the establishment of a climbing museum in Grand Teton National Park.

■ *Pete asked me if I would ever climb again, and I said probably not. That's the best way to remember it. I think the last thing I said was that I would prefer never to disgrace any pile of rocks with a bad performance.*

-XM